6·50

AN INVESTIGATION INTO GENDER DIFFERENCES IN ACHIEVEMENT

PHASE 2: School and Classroom Strategies

Laura Sukhnandan
Barbara Lee
Sara Kelleher

INVESTOR IN PEOPLE

nfer

Published in January 2000
by the National Foundation for Educational Research,
The Mere, Upton Park, Slough, Berkshire SL1 2DQ

CONTENTS

LIST OF TABLES

LIST OF ILLUSTRATIONS

ACKNOWLEDGEMENTS

We would like to take this opportunity to thank the following people who made a significant contribution to the completion of this project. To begin with we would like to thank the rest of the project team: Peter Birmingham and David Wilkinson, who helped with the fieldwork; Paula Hammond, the project statistician, and our colleagues in the NFER Library, particularly Pauline Benefield, Chris Taylor and Ellie Stephens.

We would especially like to thank all of the staff and the pupils in the case study schools who agreed to participate in the study as well as the LEA advisers who returned our pro forma and provided us with nominations of schools and the many schools that we contacted to gather further information on their strategies.

We are also grateful to the following members of our steering group for their constructive comments throughout the course of the project: Meg Buckingham (HMI), Peter Dickson (Deputy Head of Evaluation and Policy Studies, NFER), Adrian Ingham (Policy Adviser, London Borough of Hillingdon) and Alan Rawlings (Deputy Area Senior Inspector, Hampshire Inspection and Advisory Service).

Finally, we would like to express our thanks to Mrs Lack, the Headteacher of Harlyn Primary School, for allowing us to pilot our schedules in her school; Dr Marian Sainsbury for her invaluable comments on the draft report; David Upton, for his editorial comments and Enver Carim for coordinating the production of the report.

1. INTRODUCTION

1.1 The purpose of the project

In the past few years, there has been increasing concern about boys' relatively poor levels of achievement in comparison with girls. This concern has been fuelled by much media attention and speculation through headlines such as *'Girls outclassing boys'* (Carvel, 1997), *'The male liberator's sit-down protest'* (Hugill, 1998), *'Failing boys "public burden number one"'* (Dean, 1998) and *'Gender gap widens to a gulf'* (Cassidy, 1999). This has led to a wave of research which has explored three main areas: the extent of gender differences in achievement, explanations for its existence and, on the basis of these findings, the types of initiatives that schools can adopt in order to address this discrepancy.

However, there has been little research, as yet, into the level of take-up of different strategies, the rationale behind the adoption of specific strategies, how various strategies have been implemented and the extent to which the strategies have addressed gender differences in achievement.

This project, completed at the National Foundation for Educational Research (NFER), forms part of the research programme funded by the Local Government Association. The NFER project aimed to:

♦ explore the range of strategies currently operating in schools to address gender differences in achievement;

♦ identify examples of 'good practice' in this area;

♦ investigate the rationale behind schools' adoption of strategies, the way in which strategies have been implemented and the extent to which the strategies have addressed gender differences in achievement;

♦ analyse the perceived impact that these approaches have had on schools, teachers and pupils; and

♦ produce a report that will assist schools wishing to adopt similar strategies.

In order to achieve these aims, a two-phase approach was adopted. Phase 1 of the project took place between August and December 1998. Its main purpose was:

♦ to gain an overview of the main issues regarding gender differences in achievement through a review of the relevant research literature; and

♦ to gain some insight into how staff in schools were currently responding to the issue of gender differences in achievement.

Phase 2 of the study, on which this report is predominantly based, took place between January and June 1999. Its main purpose was:

♦ to investigate the rationale behind schools' adoption of specific strategies;

♦ to explore the ways in which particular types of strategies had been implemented through case studies; and

♦ to assess how effectively schools had addressed gender differences in achievement.

1.2   The purpose of this report

This report builds on the review of research and preliminary findings from Phase 1 of the project (Sukhnandan, 1999). It draws on the findings from case studies in order to describe the implementation and efficacy of particular strategies that schools have adopted to address gender differences in achievement. The report aims to inform and assist teachers by providing detailed examples of transferable strategies.

1.3   Research design

Since the 1970s, there has been a considerable amount of research into gender differences in achievement. It was decided that, for Phase 1 of the project, a review would be carried out of *recent* research that was directly relevant to this project in order to gain an overview of the main issues. In addition, in an attempt to gain some insight into how schools were responding to the issue of gender differences in achievement, a pro forma was sent to all local education authorities (LEAs) in England and Wales requesting:

(1) information about the strategies schools were currently using to address gender differences in achievement; and

(2) nominations of schools that had initiatives in place which LEAs regarded as examples of 'good practice' (see Appendix 1.1 for definition used).

The information that LEAs provided on the pro formas was analysed to find out about the strategies schools were adopting and their purpose. It is important to note that the main aim of the pro forma was to obtain from LEAs nominations of schools that had strategies in place representing examples of good practice. The findings from the analysis should therefore not be perceived as representing a comprehensive survey of the number of schools which were addressing the issue of gender differences nor of the different strategies being implemented.

The findings from the analysis of the pro forma, along with the information obtained from the general review of recent literature, were then used in Phase 2 of the study to establish a set of criteria by which to choose case study schools. It was decided to focus the case studies on the following three main areas:

♦ classroom organisation, in terms of the use of single-sex classes at secondary level;

♦ mentoring and role modelling, in terms of the use of adults from outside school, members of staff within school and other pupils, at the secondary level; and

♦ additional literacy support, in terms of the use of adult volunteers from outside school, at the primary level.

These areas were chosen because they covered a number of different strategies which the literature suggested schools were increasingly turning towards but which were relatively under-researched.

Having identified these three main areas for further investigation, 19 schools (from those nominated by LEAs) were then selected as case studies on the basis that they:

♦ had strategies in place that fell into one of the three main areas on which Phase 2 was focusing;

♦ varied in terms of: geographical location (across England and Wales); type of local authority; and context (such as urban, suburban and rural);

♦ represented different catchment areas in terms of the social background of the pupils.

Data from the 19 case study schools were obtained through:

♦ interviews with teachers, which explored: the rationale, planning and training informing the strategies; how the strategies had been implemented; and the ways in which the effects of the strategies had been evaluated;

♦ interviews exploring pupils' perceptions of the strategies;

♦ observations of the strategy in action; and

♦ the collection and analysis of relevant documentation.

1.4 The case study schools

A total of 19 schools were selected as case studies. Eight were secondary schools that had adopted single-sex classes, another eight were secondary schools that had implemented mentoring programmes and the final three were primary schools that had decided to use additional literacy supporters. A comparatively small number of primary schools were chosen for participation in the study due to concerns about the amount of pressure staff were under, at the time of the project, to implement initiatives such as the National Literacy Strategy. The 19 schools were located across England and Wales (see Table 1.1) and were in a range of different types of local education authority (see Table 1.2).

Table 1.1: The geographical location of the case study schools

	No. adopting single-sex classes	No. adopting mentoring	No. adopting adult literacy supporters	Total number
North-east	1	1	1	3
North-west	1	2	0	3
Midlands	3	2	1	6
South-east	0	1	1	2
South-west	1	1	0	2
Wales	2	1	0	3
Total	8	8	3	19

Table 1.2: The types of LEAs in which schools were located

	No. adopting single-sex classes	No. adopting mentoring	No. adopting adult literacy supporters	Total number
Metropolitan	1	3	3	7
New unitaries	4	2	0	6
Counties	1	2	0	3
Wales	2	1	0	3

Information was also collected from the schools taking part in this study on their catchment area (see Table 1.3) and the pupils catered for in terms of age range and number on roll.

The case study schools were located in a range of catchment areas, with roughly equal numbers serving rural, suburban and urban areas for schools that had adopted single-sex classes and for schools that had adopted mentoring programmes. All three of the primary schools were located in inner cities.

Of the secondary schools, roughly half of the schools catered for pupils aged 11–16 while the other half provided for pupils aged 11–18. This remained consistent for both sets of schools (those that had implemented single-sex classes and those that had implemented mentoring).

Approximately half of the schools had more than 1,000 pupils on roll whilst the others had fewer than this. Again this remained consistent for both sets of schools. Data collected on the number of pupils eligible for free school meals within the case study schools revealed that roughly half of the schools had below the national average while half had above. Again this remained consistent for both sets of schools. The majority of schools had fewer than ten per cent of pupils from ethnic minority backgrounds.

Table 1.3: The catchment area of the case study school

	No. adopting single-sex classes	No. adopting mentoring	No. adopting adult literacy supporters	Total number
Mainly country town/rural	2	3	0	5
Mainly suburban	4	3	0	7
Mainly urban/ inner-city	2	2	3	7

Of the three primary schools, roll size varied from approximately 200 to 400. They all had more than the national average number of pupils who were eligible for free school meals during 1999. Two of the schools catered for pupils from a variety of ethnic minority backgrounds while the remaining school catered for predominantly white pupils.

Within this report, pseudonyms have been used when referring to specific case study schools in order to ensure confidentiality.

1.5 Definitions and key points

Within this report, an explicit distinction has been made between the use of the words 'achievement' and 'attainment'. 'Achievement' has been used to describe progress made by pupils in the broadest sense whilst 'attainment' has been used to define gains made by pupils specifically in terms of test or examination results.

In addition, care has been taken to avoid using language that may suggest that *all* boys or *all* girls can be deemed to behave in an identical fashion.

Finally, it is also useful to recognise that research into gender differences in achievement tends to focus on trends, in order to make generalisations. However, differences at both the school level (in terms of subject areas, assessment techniques, pupil groupings, teaching methods, school ethos) and at the individual pupil level (in terms of a pupil's social background, race and personal attributes) are likely to influence and complexify the size and nature of gender differences in performance. For example, a recent study (Strand, 1999) which investigated the association between class, gender and race on the educational progress of pupils between the ages of four and seven found marked differences in attainment between groups of pupils differentiated by a combination of their sex, ethnic group and socio-economic status, although the reasons for this had yet to be fully explored.

Therefore, while generalisations about gender differences may be true at the aggregate level, they may actually be untrue or unhelpful at the individual pupil level (Arnold, 1997). It is thus unsurprising to note that the findings from studies into the causes of gender differences in achievement generally reveal that there are neither simple explanations nor 'quick-fix-solutions' for gender gaps in performance.

1.6   Report structure

An overview of the main findings from Phase 1 of this project is presented in the following chapter (Chapter 2). This includes a review of recent research on gender differences in achievement and a summary of LEA information on provision. Following an outline of the context for Phase 2 of the project, the findings from the investigation into the three strategies to address gender differences in achievement are presented. These strategies are single-sex classes (Chapter 3), mentoring (Chapter 4) and adult literacy support at the primary level (Chapter 5). Each of these chapters provides a brief background to the area of interest before outlining why these strategies were adopted, how they have been implemented and their level of effectiveness in terms of addressing gender differences in achievement. Finally, Chapter 6 highlights the main findings from this study and their implications for future research.

2. AN OVERVIEW OF FINDINGS FROM PHASE 1

This chapter summarises the main findings from Phase 1 of the study, by presenting an overview of recent research on gender differences and a summary of LEA information on provision.

2.1 An overview of recent literature

This overview of the recent research literature on gender differences will focus upon:

- the extent of gender differences in achievement;

- explanations for the existence of these differences; and

- the different types of strategies which have been proposed to address them.

The extent of gender differences and subject preferences

Over the past 30 years there has been a notable shift in the pattern of educational performance (Arnot *et al.*, 1998), from similar proportions of boys and girls obtaining five O-level passes to girls outperforming boys in virtually all subjects (Warrington and Younger, 1997; Gallagher, 1997; OFSTED and EOC, 1996). In contrast, differences in subject preferences continue to follow traditional gendered lines, with boys preferring to study science, mathematics and information technology; and girls preferring to study English, humanities and music (Gallagher, 1997; OFSTED and EOC, 1996; Arnot *et al.*, 1998; Bleach, 1998b). These gendered preferences are sustained at A-level and for subjects studied for vocational qualifications.

However, it is important to recognise, firstly, that contrary to media speculation, boys are not attaining less than in the past, but that girls are increasing their levels of attainment at a faster rate (Bray *et al.*, 1997; Warrington and Younger, 1997; Gallagher, 1997; Bleach, 1998a). It is therefore worthwhile remembering that both boys' and girls' levels of attainment have increased over time (Gallagher, 1997).

Secondly, researchers (Arnot *et al.*, 1998; Raphael Reed, 1998; Bleach, 1998a) have stated that it is essential that gender differences in achievement are not seen in isolation but are considered in relation to factors such as social class and race.

Finally, it is important to recognise that changes in educational policy have had the effect of placing not only pupil achievement into the consciousness of the general public, but also gender differences in achievement and thus girls' outperformance of boys. Consequently, media attention and speculation can be said to have fuelled public interest and concern over this issue.

Explaining gender differences in attainment

The findings from the literature on reasons for gender differences in attainment can be divided into two main strands:

(1) school – related factors, such as changes in curriculum content and assessment procedures, teacher – pupil relations, pupil subcultures, and pupil attitudes and behaviour; and

(2) out-of-school factors, such as biological influences, the process of socialisation and the effect of social change in late twentieth century Britain.

School-related factors

It can be argued that recent changes in curriculum content and assessment procedures can provide some explanation for girls' outperformance of boys over the last decade. The introduction of the National Curriculum meant that all pupils had to study the same core subjects. A higher number of pupils were therefore entered for examinations as they all studied courses which led to GCSEs. This resulted in a decrease in the gender 'entry gap' in most subjects (Arnot *et al.,* 1998) and enabled girls to compete with boys in subjects which had previously given boys an advantage in higher education and the workplace (Warrington and Younger, 1997; Pickering, 1997).

There is a considerable amount of research (Bleach, 1998b; Murphy and Elwood, 1996; OFSTED and EOC, 1996; Arnot *et al.,* 1998) that has investigated girls' and boys' preferences and interaction with curriculum content. Such work has found that girls' preferred style of written response is extended, reflective composition. Girls are therefore more successful in reflective aspects of their work (Murphy and Elwood, 1996; OFSTED and EOC, 1996) and do better on sustained tasks that are open-ended, process-based and related to realistic situations (Arnot *et al.,* 1998).

In contrast, boys have narrower experiences of fiction (Bleach, 1998b). Their preferred style of written response is factual and commentative (Murphy and Elwood, 1996). Boys' preferences include memorising abstract, unambiguous facts and they are often willing to sacrifice deep understanding for correct answers achieved at speed (Arnot *et al.,* 1998; Bleach, 1998b). Their learning tends to improve when they become convinced of the value in what they are doing (OFSTED and EOC, 1996).

The introduction of GCSEs and G/NVQs led to a shift from an emphasis on learning in terms of the acquisition of knowledge towards an emphasis on the process of learning (Arnot *et al.,* 1998). As a result, terminal examinations counted for less and more marks were given for the ability to be analytical rather than speculative within coursework (Warrington and Younger, 1997; Pickering, 1997). It has been argued that this increased element of continuous learning favoured the more sequential learning of girls (Warrington and Younger, 1997; Pickering, 1997; Arnold, 1997; Bleach, 1998b).

It is interesting to note, however, that the changes in the criteria for GCSEs in 1993 – 94, which reduced the amount of coursework that was required, did not immediately reduce the superiority of girls' performance (OFSTED and EOC, 1996). Therefore, although some evidence shows that girls do slightly better on the coursework elements of assessment, this may only marginally affect pupils' overall results (Arnot *et al.*, 1998). Furthermore, evidence has also revealed that girls outperform boys in both coursework and exams (NEAB, 1996).

Teachers' gender values and expectations of, and behaviour towards, boys and girls have also been found to play an important role in shaping pupils' perceptions of, and reactions to, school (Arnot *et al.*, 1998). Research has shown that boys are more likely than girls to explicitly challenge the authority of the teacher (Warrington and Younger, 1997). In addition, because boys' contributions are physically and verbally more prominent, they more frequently have their contributions evaluated by teachers and peers – both positively and negatively (Arnot *et al.*, 1998). Teachers are thus seen as more hostile towards boys (for example, as 'picking on' boys) by all children (Warrington and Younger, 1997; Pickering, 1997), which can have detrimental effects on the attitudes of boys towards school and learning. Interestingly, few teachers acknowledge the possibility that they treat girls and boys differently in the classroom (Warrington and Younger, 1997; Pickering, 1997).

Some research (Bray *et al.*, 1997; Pickering, 1997; Gallagher, 1997) suggests that there is an anti-intellectual, anti-educational and anti-learning culture amongst boys. It has been suggested that because boys come into contact mainly with women in their formative years they see few role models of successful men at home and in the school (Pickering, 1997; Bleach, 1998b), which may affect their beliefs about adult roles (OFSTED and EOC, 1996). Commentators (Pickering, 1997; Bleach, 1998b) have thus suggested that boys may develop an anti-school subculture because an important component of masculinity is avoidance of what is feminine. Boys therefore develop the belief that a positive attitude towards schooling, the choice of female subjects and overt involvement and engagement in school and learning is effeminate and thus at odds with the development of their masculine identity (Cohen, 1998). In this way, the pressure to conform to the gender stereotype of not working and opting for 'male' subjects is immense. In contrast, girls have rarely been negatively labelled for achieving (Gallagher, 1997; Cohen, 1998) or because of their subject choices.

Providing further evidence to support this claim, it has been found that boys and girls have notably different orientations towards schoolwork and learning which may contribute to gender differences in performance. (Arnot *et al.,* 1998; Bleach, 1998b; Bray *et al.,* 1997; OFSTED and EOC, 1996; Warrington and Younger, 1997). Girls have high aspirations and they value presentation and clear expression. They tend to underestimate their own ability and therefore work hard to try and compensate. Girls spend more time on their homework because they want to achieve high standards and please their teachers (Bray *et al.,* 1997; OFSTED and EOC, 1996).

In contrast, boys prefer active learning and tend to be over-confident and to overestimate their own ability (Bray *et al.,* 1997; OFSTED and EOC, 1996; Bleach, 1998b). They have less positive attitudes towards schoolwork and homework, are less attentive in class and are more reluctant to do extra work (Warrington and Younger, 1997; Pickering, 1997; Gallagher, 1997; OFSTED and EOC, 1996).

Out-of school-factors

Some commentators have suggested that gender differences in attainment can be attributed to the genetic differences that exist between boys and girls. For example, it has been argued that because girls mature physically more rapidly than boys, this may account for their more developed personal and social behaviour (OFSTED and EOC, 1996). However, it has been noted that biological explanations fail to provide an adequate explanation for changes in the trends of boys' and girls' attainment over time (Gallagher, 1997).

Researchers (Murphy and Elwood, 1996, 1998; Arnot *et al.,* 1998; Bleach, 1998b) investigating the impact of socialisation have noted that boys and girls are socialised, from birth, towards particular roles, often based on adult interpretations of appropriate and inappropriate behaviours. These expectations set in train different patterns of development which manifest themselves in playgroups and extend through the early years of primary school.

Girls are socialised to listen and pay attention, to play without supervision and to establish their own rules and roles. By secondary level, they are characterised as having a 'compliant, motivational style' (Bleach, 1998b), whereas boys are socialised to be noisy, attention-seeking and at seven years old find it difficult to sit still and pay attention. By secondary school, they want to do everything quickly, prefer short-term tasks and identify with 'macho' values, which can lead them to regard studious behaviour as unmanly and, on occasion, to result in disruptive and threatening behaviour (Bleach, 1998b).

These different experiences of socialisation inevitably lead boys and girls to adopt different interests, pastimes and hobbies from an early age; these activities provide them with different language opportunities and align them in different ways to schooling and learning (Murphy and Elwood, 1998). These differential interests (such as preferences for particular types of books) are then exploited within schools. The effect of this is to encourage boys and girls to continue focusing on limited aspects of their environment, leading to the development of particular skills.

At a broader level, it can be argued that social changes that have occurred in Britain over the last 20 – 30 years can also help to explain the gender gap. These include the introduction of comprehensive schooling and the demise of the 11+ (Epstein *et al.*, 1998), equal opportunity initiatives during the 1980s (Gallagher, 1997) and the labour market changes during the 1980s which led to the disappearance of apprenticeships and on-the-job training, which disproportionately affected (working-class) males (Arnot *et al.*, 1998). Whilst some boys have been able to adapt to the new vocational/curriculum opportunities, it has been argued that labour market changes may have helped create a group of 'macho' lads, who are unmotivated and unwilling to learn.

Strategies for addressing gender differences

On the basis of the explanations cited, a number of strategies have been identified as possible ways of addressing the current discrepancies in achievement. These strategies can be divided into four main approaches:

1. A change to teaching methods and classroom organisation to engage pupils' interests, work with pupils' strengths and correct their perceived weaknesses. This approach includes the use of curriculum content and resources which interest both boys and girls, more teacher-led work, mixed gender pairing, single-sex grouping and the provision of learning support. It has also been advocated that learning styles are developed which give boys and girls the opportunity to appreciate the value of different ways of working and communicating for different purposes (Murphy and Elwood, 1998).

2. An improvement in teacher – pupil relations through raising staff awareness; developing and implementing whole-school policies which cover all aspects of work and behaviour; and monitoring classroom dynamics in terms of pupil – teacher interaction, levels of attention and support, levels of encouragement and teacher expectations and use of discipline.

3. Addressing the negative impact of school subcultures and poor attitudes towards school and learning by encouraging a more mature attitude towards work and by creating a culture where male students can achieve without fear of ridicule and where disruptive behaviour is not allowed to undermine the learning (Warrington and Younger, 1997; Pickering, 1997).

4. The use of other pupils, staff and people from the local community as role models and mentors for pupils, in order to address ideological changes to men's position and role in society. A number of commentators have, however, noted that care should be taken to ensure that male role models/mentors are not used to reinforce the notion of gender superiority (Pickering, 1997) and thus undermine the integrity of female teachers (Raphael Reed, 1998) but to challenge gendered stereotypes.

Researchers (Arnot *et al.*, 1998) have, however, noted that before LEAs and schools take the decision to implement practical strategies, they should analyse performance data so that they can:

♦ identify patterns of underachievement;

♦ consider other areas where gender differences occur (e.g. rate of exclusions, attendance levels);

♦ target groups of pupils at risk; and

♦ isolate the factors which contribute to gender differences .

Once strategies have been implemented, Arnot *et al.* (1998) suggest that schools should carefully monitor and evaluate their impact within schools and the local context in order to ensure that the strategies are addressing the needs of the school (OFSTED and EOC, 1996).

2.2 A summary of LEA information on provision

A primary aim of Phase 1 of this project was to identify the strategies currently operating in schools to address gender differences in achievement.

Initially, a pro forma was sent to appropriate personnel in all LEAs in England and Wales. Information was requested on:

♦ the extent to which strategies for addressing gender differences in achievement had been adopted by schools within the LEA; and

♦ the strategies that had been adopted, such as whether they were LEA- or school-based, when they had been implemented and the groups of pupils and subject areas they targeted.

LEAs were also asked to nominate schools which had been successful in addressing gender differences in achievement.

A total of 97, out of 175 LEAs (55 per cent) returned the completed pro forma and the information they provided was analysed statistically. This section of the report highlights the main findings from the analysis of the pro forma.

Main findings

Of the responding LEAs, the majority (86 per cent) were aware of strategies that were currently in operation in schools. They reported that a number of different approaches had been adopted by LEAs and schools which included:

♦ staff training;

♦ policy development;

♦ target setting;

♦ role modelling/mentoring;

♦ new teaching methods;

♦ classroom organisation (such as single-sex grouping);

♦ parental involvement; and

♦ learning support.

The whole-school initiatives, such as policy development, staff training, target setting and new teaching methods, had usually been developed at the LEA level. In contrast, the strategies most frequently adopted at school level tended to focus on classroom organisation practices and teaching methods. The four most popular school-based strategies were, therefore, single-sex grouping, role modelling/mentoring, new forms of class organisation and new teaching methods.

The majority of the strategies reported had only been implemented relatively recently. The analysis revealed that 60 per cent of the strategies were implemented during 1997 – 1998, 14 per cent during 1995 – 1996 and just four per cent prior to 1995.

Of the strategies reported, 40 per cent targeted pupils at the secondary level, 17 per cent targeted pupils at the primary level and 29 per cent targeted pupils at both the primary and secondary level. The types of strategies adopted by schools varied according to the level of school in which they were to be used. The three strategies which were most frequently reported to be in use at the primary level were: new teaching methods, parental involvement and role modelling/mentoring. Role modelling/mentoring, staff training and single-sex grouping were the strategies adopted at the secondary level.

The majority of the strategies (55 per cent) implemented to address gender differences targeted both boys and girls. Of these strategies, the three reported to be most frequently in use were policy development, target setting and staff training. It should be noted, however, that 31 per cent of the strategies were targeted specifically at boys. Of these strategies, the three reported to be most frequently in use were staff training, role modelling/ mentoring and new teaching methods. These trends, for strategies targeted at all pupils and for those targeted specifically at boys, remain consistent at both the primary and secondary level.

The analysis revealed that 39 per cent of the strategies reported were implemented at the cross-curricular and extra-curricular level. However, a third of the strategies were implemented for the core subjects, in either a combination of subjects or in individual subjects. The strategies most frequently adopted for core subjects were new teaching methods, single-sex grouping and target setting. It was also interesting to note that 29 per cent of the strategies that targeted boys only, compared with 20 per cent of strategies which targeted both boys and girls, focused specifically on English.

2.3 Summary

The findings from Phase 1 of the project revealed that many of the strategies adopted by LEAs and schools reflect those advocated by researchers who have investigated the possible causes for gender differences in achievement and ways in which to address the differences. The information summarised in this chapter formed the context for Phase 2 of this project, which involved exploring the extent to which three particular strategies were successfully addressing gender differences and the impact they were having upon those involved.

3. SINGLE-SEX CLASSES

3.1 Setting the context

There has been a great deal of research into the advantages and disadvantages of single-sex schooling compared to coeducational schooling. In brief, single-sex schooling is said to provide girls with a more favourable learning experience by protecting them from limiting traditional expectations of what are appropriate female roles (Faulkner, 1991; Mahony, 1985) and by encouraging them to follow non-traditional subject and career paths (Fisher, 1994). It is also argued that single-sex schooling provides girls with more teacher attention and increases teachers' expectations of girls (Fisher, 1994; Marjoram, 1994). In contrast, coeducational schools are seen as more appropriate in terms of enabling pupils to mix with, and relate more easily to, the opposite sex (Faulkner, 1991; Pimenoff, 1995).

In terms of pupil achievement, studies that have compared the effects of single-sex schooling with those of coeducational schooling have, on the whole, failed to find any evidence that supports one form of organisation over the other, regardless of subject area (see Dale; 1969, 1971, 1974; Bell, 1990). Consequently, a number of researchers (Smithers and Robinson, 1995; Robinson and Smithers, 1999) have suggested that the often publicised good performance of single-sex schools in examinations, in comparison with coeducational schools, is not a consequence of single-sex schooling *per se*, but is mainly due to associated factors. These factors include: the ability of the intake; the social class background of pupils; the type of school involved; and the history and tradition of the schools. Researchers (Robinson and Smithers, 1999; Steedman, 1984, 1985; Daly, 1996) in this field have argued that when these factors are controlled for, the academic differences between pupils in single-sex schools and those in mixed schools are, in general, neither significant nor conclusive.

> *When, as far as possible, like is compared with like, the apparent academic differences between single-sex and coeducational schools largely disappear.* (Robinson and Smithers, 1999, p.23)

With regard to pupils' social experiences, researchers have suggested that mixed-sex systems perpetuate traditional expectations of what constitutes appropriate male and female roles, thereby producing an atmosphere that disadvantages girls. Faulkner (1991) found that pupils from single-sex schools were significantly less negative towards the concept of female achievement than pupils from coed schools. In addition, girls from single-sex schools were significantly less traditional than their counterparts in the coed system in terms of their attitudes towards women's rights and their roles in society. Confirming these findings, Stables' (1990) study of third-year (Year 9) secondary school pupils' attitudes to science, physics, chemistry, biology and to school found that there was greater polarisation of feelings towards certain school subjects in mixed schools, especially by boys. Stables concluded:

> *subject interest and specialisation may be guided to a greater extent by a desire to conform to a received sexual stereotype in mixed schools than in single-sex schools, thus effectively narrowing career choice for coeducated pupils* (p.229).

Since the 1960s, there has been a steady and noticeable decline in the number of single-sex schools in Britain (Robinson and Smithers, 1999). Yet, in recent years, there has been a significant increase in the use of single-sex grouping and single-sex classes in mixed schools, even though there has been relatively little research into its effects. Rowe (1988) noted that

> *the movement to institute single-sex classes seems to be growing faster than the evidence to support its substantive educational justification* (p.182).

This chapter attempts to bridge this gap by presenting some evidence on the effects of single-sex classes. It draws on the findings from eight case study schools, examining their reasons for adopting single-sex classes, the means by which these classes were implemented and the effect these classes had on key participants.

3.2 Rationale for adopting single-sex classes to address gender differences in achievement

This section explains the reasons behind schools' decisions to address gender differences in achievement, the rationale for adopting single-sex classes as a strategy and the achievements which staff hoped for.

Within the case study schools, interviews with staff revealed that they were aware of increasing national concern with, and debates regarding, the relatively low levels of achievement of boys in comparison with girls. However, the impetus which led staff to consider implementing changes within their own schools was a recognition that they had a gender gap in performance, either at the whole-school level, or within individual departments. This recognition generally arose out of investigations into underachievement through statistical analyses of examination results (such as National Curriculum assessment tests and GCSEs). On occasion, it came through an awareness of gender differences in the take-up of certain options at KS4 (such as the relatively low number of girls compared with boys opting for design and technology) and gender differences in the allocation of pupils to particular sets, with boys tending to dominate the bottom sets and girls the top sets.

It can be argued that staff were motivated to investigate gender differences within their schools because of the growing national focus on gender gaps in performance, and because schools are judged (through league tables) in terms of this rather narrow definition of achievement.

Why adopt single-sex classes?

Staff at the case study schools provided a number of reasons to justify their decision to implement single-sex classes as opposed to any other strategy. Staff provided different explanations for their choice of single-sex classes depending on how gender differences had manifested themselves within their schools, in terms of the subject area, the year group and the ability level of pupils. Overall, it was possible to identify four main explanations for why staff decided to adopt single-sex classes.

Firstly, staff across many of the schools noted that an important consideration in their choice of a strategy was whether it would benefit some pupils (such as boys) at the expense of others (such as girls). Single-sex classes were therefore often adopted because many staff believed that they would not have a negative effect on those pupils that it did not target directly:

> *We thought by looking at boys and teaching them as a whole group we would be able to achieve results for boys without having the girls' results suffer.* (project coordinator)

Secondly, it has been argued that single-sex classes can be used to challenge pupils' traditional, stereotypical perceptions of the gendered nature of certain subjects by improving their perceptions and attitudes, as well as their levels of self-esteem and confidence in 'non-traditional' subjects. For example, Arnot *et al.* (1998) suggest that single-sex classes can be used to improve boys' perceptions, and consequently their performance, in subjects that are often perceived as 'feminine', such as English and modern foreign languages. Similarly, these researchers claim that single-sex classes can be seen as a way of enabling girls to enhance their competence in, and thus the numbers opting for, 'masculine' subjects such as mathematics, science and design and technology.

Staff in over half of the case study schools stated that these issues were considered important in their decision to implement single-sex classes. Staff within a number of these schools felt that by tackling pupils' traditional perceptions of certain subjects, especially those of boys, they would also be able to challenge the anti-learning subculture that many teachers felt were prevalent among some boys. A teacher at one school stated:

> *We felt that in this school, boys had some form of inferiority complex. We wanted to overcome the culture that states they cannot be seen to be successful without losing their street cred.* (headteacher)

Traditionally, the separation of boys and girls into single-sex schools was considered beneficial because it enabled schools to challenge traditional expectations of appropriate female roles, which were often seen as having an adverse effect on the potential and thus achievement of girls. However, given the present climate where girls are outperforming boys, arguably because boys perceive certain subjects as 'feminine' and are prone to adopt an anti-learning subculture, it could be suggested that the move towards single-sex classes is now enabling schools to challenge traditional expectations of appropriate male roles, which are seen as having an adverse effect on boys.

A third reason, provided by staff within three of the case study schools, for adopting single-sex classes was that teachers felt they offered the best practical solution, given issues such as the hierarchical nature of the subject under focus (for example mathematics), and the constraints of class sizes and school timetables:

> *It seemed sensible to address the issue by looking at the grouping of pupils because it was easy for us to move the pupils around due to them being in the same timetable block.* (subject teacher)

Finally, taking a broader outlook, Daly (1996) suggests that the move towards the implementation of single-sex classes/grouping has occurred because

> *in the context of growing political commitment to parental consumer demands regarding public education services, single-sex schooling is an organisational issue* (p. 302).

Confirming, to some extent, Daly's suggestion, senior members of staff at one of the case study schools admitted that although they had implemented single-sex classes in more than one year group and more than one subject primarily to encourage teachers to look at the process of teaching and learning, they also saw it as a 'unique selling point' for the school, given the current national emphasis on parental choice.

What schools hoped to achieve

Staff within the case study schools hoped that by implementing single-sex classes, they would be able to achieve certain aims. These targets inevitably varied according to the way in which gender differences had manifested themselves within the different schools. At a general level, staff at two schools hoped that single-sex classes would simply help to reduce the gender gap in achievement. However, staff at four schools implemented single-sex classes specifically to target pupils who had the ability to achieve five or more GCSEs at grade A – C but were at risk of not fulfilling their potential. These teachers hoped that by focusing on these pupils, the majority of whom were boys, they would be able to both address gender differences in achievement and improve overall pupil performance at GCSE.

At a more specific level, staff at one school hoped that single-sex classes would help to increase the number of girls opting for design and technology at KS4 while staff at another school hoped that these classes would lead to an increase in the number of boys being allocated to the higher sets in modern foreign languages at KS4.

Staff within all of the case study schools stated that the ultimate aim for the adoption and implementation of single-sex classes was that it would improve pupil performance in GCSE examinations, usually in terms of the number of A – C grades.

3.3 Use of single-sex classes

The strategies in the case study schools had all been implemented relatively recently. Those that dated back to 1996 had often been modified and were running smoothly. Many of the schools were still in the pilot stage, having only phased in the classes during 1997 and 1998.

Across the schools, single-sex classes were implemented in different subject areas for different year groups and for pupils of different ability levels in relation to the aims held by staff for adopting them. Table 3.3 below summarises the areas that case study schools focused upon.

Table 3.3: Pupils targeted for single-sex classes.

School	Subject(s) targeted	Year group targeted	Ability set targeted
Applewood Comp.	English	Y10 and 11	Lower band
Blackberry Hill	English	Y10 and 11	Y10: middle & low / Y11: all
Cherrytree High	English	Y10 and 11	Middle sets
Dewberry Street	English	Y10 and 11	Middle sets
	Design and technology	Y9	Mixed-ability sets
Elderfield High	English	Y8	Mixed-ability sets
Foxton Comp.	Modern foreign languages	Y8	High sets
Greengage School	Mathematics	Y10 and 11	Middle sets
Honeyfield School	All subjects	Y8 – 10	All sets

In a recent review of research on gender differences in achievement, Arnot *et al.* (1998) found that the two main areas where gender gaps were most prominent among compulsory-age pupils were in early literacy skills/ English and GCSE examination performance – where girls outperformed boys. Reflecting these concerns, in six of the case study schools, staff decided to implement these classes in language-based subjects, primarily English but also modern foreign languages. Other subject areas targeted by the case study schools included mathematics and design and technology, and at one case study school, single-sex classes were implemented in all subject areas.

Mahony (1998) has argued that the move towards a market-led education system has resulted in a narrowing of the definition and measurement of achievement to the number of five or more A – C grades at GCSE. This has increased pressure on schools to pour resources into supporting pupils who are underachieving according to this criterion. This approach implies that schools may not actually be targeting those pupils who are underachieving to the greatest extent, such as pupils of high or low ability, simply because increased achievement amongst these groups would not impact as significantly on the overall performance level of schools in terms of the number of five or more A – C grades at GCSE.

It is not, therefore, surprising that in six of the case study schools, pupils who were at KS4 – the GCSE examination years – were targeted. In order to decide on which subgroup of pupils within the year group to target, staff at five of these schools used a combination of test results, examination predictions and teacher judgement. As a result, they were able to identify the groups of pupils which were most at risk of underachieving. Consequently, of these five schools, three focused on middle-ability pupils, one on low-ability pupils and one on all pupils (due to the disproportionate number of boys and girls within the year group). Illustration 3.1 below describes the process that staff at one school went through in order to identify their target population.

Illustration 3.1: How staff identified their target population

At Greengage School, the project coordinator (PC) began the identification of the target pupils by analysing the NCA results of all Year 9 pupils. From this analysis the PC identified all pupils who had achieved two to three Level 5s, which the PC felt provided a general indication that these pupils had the potential to achieve five or more A – C grades at GCSE. For the identified Year 9 pupils, the PC asked subject teachers to give each pupil an optimistic and a pessimistic examination grade. The gulf between these predictions for the boys was greater than it was for the girls, which suggested that the boys were at a greater risk of underachieving. Staff within the mathematics department looked at the sets that these boys were in and realised that they were located within the middle sets. They therefore took the decision to target these boys by converting the middle two sets into two single-sex classes.

Staff at three of the case study schools stated that whilst they wanted to address gender differences in achievement or in the take-up of options, they felt that the best way to achieve this was to try and address the issue at the root of the problem. Staff consequently opted to implement single-sex classes at KS3.

For example, at Foxton Comprehensive, staff decided to implement single-sex classes for Year 8, high-ability pupils in MFL. They believed that by taking this approach, they would be able to address the negative attitudes and perceptions that some able boys held towards MFL, which staff felt had an adverse impact on their levels of achievement as these pupils moved up the school. Staff hoped that this would then help to increase the number of boys who were allocated to the top sets when they reached KS4, thus reducing the gender gap in achievement in MFL at GCSE.

At Dewberry Street, staff decided to use single-sex classes in design and technology for all Year 9 pupils regardless of ability (pupils were put into mixed-ability classes). Staff at this school hoped that by taking this approach, they would be able to improve girls' perceptions and attitudes towards design and technology and thus increase the number of girls opting for design and technology at KS4, thereby addressing gender differences in option choices.

3.4 The process of implementation

This section describes the process that staff within the case study schools went through in order to implement single-sex classes. It covers the practical preparations made, the training provided to staff, the funding required to get the strategy operational and the different types of difficulties that staff faced.

Practical preparations

Within seven of the case study schools, few practical preparations had to be made in order to implement single-sex classes. These schools used a blocked timetable system and because they were generally targeting specific sets within a year group, were able to simply combine targeted sets and convert them into single-sex classes, enabling timetables to remain unchanged. One school, however, had to make significant changes to its timetable as senior management had decided to implement single-sex classes across more than one year group in a number of different subject areas.

In terms of resources, staff across the case study schools generally reported that few additional resources were required. However, staff in some of the schools that implemented single-sex classes in English stated that additional curriculum materials such as books which specifically targeted boys did have to be acquired.

Staff training

In over half of the case study schools, staff were not provided with any form of training prior to, or following, the implementation of single-sex classes. Project coordinators argued that this was either because single-sex classes had only been implemented at an experimental level, and they believed that teachers needed to obtain first-hand experience before receiving training; or because they felt that their teachers were experienced enough to adjust to the new form of pupil grouping without additional training. On the whole, subject teachers within these schools generally agreed with this approach, although, some staff noted that if they had been asked to teach all-boy classes, they would have like to have received some training. Those staff within these schools who were allocated to teach all-boy classes were usually project coordinators who were well informed about single-sex classes and therefore did not necessarily feel that specific training was necessary.

Within a few of the schools, staff did receive training on approaches to teaching single-sex classes, in terms of teaching methods and curriculum materials. At some schools, staff received formal training which was led by either project coordinators or educational consultants, whilst at other schools, staff were provided with informal training through a variety of different channels. For example, at some schools, staff simply had discussions with other members of staff within the department (including the project coordinator) about ways of teaching single-sex classes, whilst at other schools, staff received information about single-sex classes that was cascaded to them by the project coordinator. In general, staff within these schools found that the training provided, whether formal or informal, was valuable in terms of preparing them to teach single-sex classes. At one school, however, where the cascading of information had failed to work effectively, some staff were left feeling uninformed, uninvolved and unprepared.

Funding

In general, the implementation of single-sex classes had not cost schools significant amounts of money. As mentioned previously, some of the schools that were focusing on English had to obtain funding to buy the additional curriculum materials that they needed, but this was usually obtained through the departmental budget rather than the school budget or external agencies. A few schools drew on the school budget to fund INSET. The only other costs mentioned were those required to cover the time of the project coordinator, which were also minimal.

Difficulties encountered

Staff within all of the case study schools were very positive about their experiences of implementing single-sex classes and very few highlighted any difficulties. This was partly because in many of the case study schools, the initiatives were still at an early stage and were seen as an experiment, something to try and modify until the most suitable strategy for the targeted pupils was found:

> *You must be prepared to experiment and adapt a strategy before it can be fully implemented – that is what has been the key here ... there is never a way of knowing how it is going to be received so we started with one year group and implemented it to cover all of KS4 the following year.* (subject teacher)

3.5 Teachers and teaching

This section describes the roles and responsibilities that key members of staff took in the implementation of single-sex classes. It then explains how staff were selected to teach single-sex classes and the ways in which these teachers modified their teaching methods to accommodate these classes. The section finally presents teachers' perceptions of the use of single-sex classes in terms of its impact on their role as a teacher and in terms of its effect on teacher – pupil relations.

Staff roles and responsibilities

Overall, once senior management became aware that there was a gender gap in achievement within the school, they often decided to address it by implementing whole-school initiatives, within which individual departments were given responsibility for tackling the gap in their own subject area. Within individual departments, a designated member of staff was usually given the job of conducting preliminary research into the issue to identify the groups of pupils which were affected, the likely causes of the gender gap and possible strategies for addressing it. This was often done by researching or reading around the topic or by discussions with members of staff who had previous experience of tackling gender differences. Staff at a couple of the schools stated that information was obtained though their LEA, although none of the case study schools which had implemented single-sex classes were actually in LEA initiatives to address gender differences in achievement at that time.

The findings of this preliminary research were then presented to the department and staff decided on the best plan of action. Project coordinators within most of the schools noted that it was important for the success of the project that all members of staff within the department were able to take an active part in the decision-making process. Once staff had agreed on a strategy, the department obtained confirmation and support from the SMT, the school governors and, in some cases, parents before commencing with implementation.

The main role of the project coordinator was to organise the implementation of the classes, liaise with key members of staff and to monitor and evaluate the effectiveness of the strategy. Departmental staff all took an active part in the decision-making process to implement single-sex classes and were also involved in discussions on how it was working. In general, only a few teachers were directly involved in teaching single-sex classes and therefore required to modify their approaches accordingly (see section on *Teaching strategies* below).

In most of the case study schools, headteachers often acknowledged that their role in the implementation of the strategy was to provide support and encouragement with little direct intervention. Staff from other departments not directly involved with implementing single-sex classes rarely had anything more than a general understanding of how single-sex classes were being used.

The project coordinators in roughly half of the case study schools stated that although implementing single-sex classes was initially labour intensive, it had not added significantly to their workload because it was often part of their overall responsibilities. However, the remaining project coordinators had felt that the implementation of single-sex classes had impacted to some degree on their workloads.

In contrast, the subject teachers interviewed in all of the schools generally reported that they did not think that single-sex classes had made a significant impact on their workload. Some of the teachers noted that any increase in workload that had occurred since the implementation of single-sex classes was primarily due to the wider range of ability within the single-sex classes (see *The impact of single-sex classes on class composition* below).

The allocation of staff to single-sex classes

Staff were allocated to all-boy or all-girl classes on the basis of one of the following four factors: teacher gender; to ensure that teachers were able to maintain contact with both boys and girls; teacher interest in taking single-sex classes; and for reasons of practicality.

For example, in three of the schools that had implemented single-sex classes in language-based subjects, staff stated that they tried to allocate male teachers to their all-boy classes so that the male subject teacher could act as a positive role model for the boys. Staff considered this necessary because they believed that boys had a tendency to perceive language-based subjects as 'feminine', a notion that was often reinforced by the fact that these subjects were predominantly taught by women. Staff therefore felt that if these boys could see a male teacher teaching language-based subjects, their perceptions of these subjects might improve and have a positive impact upon their levels of achievement in these subject areas.

However, a number of researchers (Raphael Reed, 1998; Pickering, 1997) have noted that the use of male role models to challenge boys' negative perceptions of 'feminine' subjects may actually undermine the integrity of female teachers and reinforce the notion of gender superiority.

A model which seemed to take more account of that concern was adopted by Greengage School, which had implemented single-sex classes in mathematics. Staff decided to rotate the male and female subject teachers between the all-boy and the all-girl classes. This allowed the same teacher to teach both the boys and girls the same topic and enabled them to maintain contact with all of the pupils, countering any apprehensions that they had about teaching just boys or just girls, having originally chosen to work in a coeducational school. By implementing this system of teacher rotation, the project coordinator was also able to monitor the impact of single-sex classes without having to make allowances for the effect of different teachers.

Within two case study schools, it was decided that the best approach was to ask teachers to volunteer to take either the all-boy or the all-girl class, whilst in the remaining two schools, subject teachers were simply allocated to single-sex classes on the basis of practicalities in terms of timetabling.

The impact of single-sex classes on class composition

Within all of the case study schools, staff had to make concessions in the way that they set pupils in order to implement single-sex classes. At most of the schools, staff noted that this compromise had a number of implications. Firstly, grouping pupils into single-sex classes meant that classes tended to contain pupils with a wider range of ability than they would otherwise have had. As a result, teachers found that they had to do more preparation, differentiate to a greater degree and use a wider range of textbooks in order to meet the needs of their wider-ability single-sex class. Some teachers consequently found single-sex classes more difficult to teach. Furthermore, some felt that the lower-ability pupils within their class found it more difficult to learn as many were under pressure to keep up with the rest of the class, which, especially for some of the boys, appeared to have a demoralising effect.

Secondly, depending on the number of boys and girls within a year group, the implementation of single-sex classes for particular ability groups, sometimes led to uneven class sizes, especially when pupils with special educational needs were withdrawn for extra support, as these pupils tended predominantly to be boys.

Despite the impact of single-sex classes on setting processes, a small number of teachers felt that the 'trade-off' had been worthwhile. For example, a number of English and MFL teachers noted that setting pupils solely by ability often led to an over-representation of girls in the top sets and an over-representation of boys in the bottom sets. However, the majority of teachers felt that it was too early to assess whether single-sex classes would lead to greater achievements than setting pupils by ability.

Teaching strategies

In recent years, there has been a considerable amount of research (Murphy and Elwood, 1996; OFSTED and EOC, 1996; Arnot *et al.*, 1998) which has revealed that, overall, boys and girls interact with curriculum content differently and favour different teaching and learning styles. One of the main advantages of single-sex classes is that they allow teachers to modify their teaching methods and curriculum materials to suit the different learning styles and preferences of boys and girls. Teachers who adopt this approach, therefore, hope that it will enable them to raise pupils' levels of motivation, thus facilitating the learning process and ultimately improving pupils' levels of achievement.

In this study, teachers in most of the schools that had implemented single-sex classes considered it important to tailor their teaching methods to the gender of the class. However, the changes that they made tended to be in relation to the all-boy classes rather than the all-girl classes, especially in language-based subjects. This was because many teachers believed that the teaching methods and curriculum materials currently used in language-based lessons tended to favour the learning styles of girls and therefore only needed to be adjusted for the all-boy classes.

The kinds of modifications adopted by teachers for all-boy classes tended to focus on making lessons very structured. They provided the boys with a succession of short-term tasks that had clear targets. Lessons also tended to be taught on a whole-class basis which allowed the teacher to interact directly with the boys for greater periods of time and to keep the pace of the lesson brisk. In contrast, all-girl classes were characterised by greater pupil autonomy, small-group work and long-term goals:

> *I've found boys respond best to being given short tasks and set targets for each lesson. With the girls I've found I can leave them to get on with just one long task for the whole of the lesson. I allow the girls to organise themselves much more and to direct their own pace of learning with minimum teacher input.*
>
> (subject teacher)

See illustrations 3.2 and 3.3 for examples of how teachers modified their lessons to cater for single-sex classes.

Illustration 3.2: An example of a lesson for an all-boy class

At Applewood School, a Year 11 all-boy, bottom set (n=9), English lesson was observed. The 50-minute lesson was very structured. The teacher used whole-class teaching and a variety of short-term tasks. The lesson also included a range of teaching methods based on the use of competition.

Before the lesson began, the boys lined up outside the classroom and the teacher checked that they were in uniform before they were allowed to enter in silence, sit down in rows facing the front, and take out their books. The actual lesson began with a question-and-answer session, which reviewed the work done in the previous lesson. The teacher would ask a question and the boys would put their hands up to answer. The teacher then chose five boys and numbered them one to five before asking them, in turn, what their answers were. The class then read from a book where the teacher read one paragraph and would then choose a boy, from those who put their hands up, to read the next paragraph. This was followed by another question-and-answer session, based on what had been read. This session followed the same structure as the one at the beginning of the lesson. The pupils then did a role play based on what they had read. The subject teacher asked the boys to volunteer to be different characters from the book. In order to decide, from the number of volunteers, who would have the part, the teacher would turn it into a race and the first boy to put his hand up from resting it on the desk would get the part. In the last five minutes, the subject teacher summed up the new ideas that the boys had learnt and did another quickfire question-and-answer session. He dismissed the boys, who left quietly.

Throughout the lesson, the boys sat in silence, listening and paying attention, unless they were answering a question. They all took an active part throughout the lesson with practically every pupil putting his hand up to volunteer an answer at every opportunity. The boys appeared to enjoy the lesson and were not embarrassed to take risks answering questions or reading aloud to the class.

This illustration has been used to highlight some of the ways in which teachers modified their approaches when teaching all-boy classes such as by having a highly structured lesson, introducing an element of competition and keeping the pace of the lesson brisk. Teachers within the case study schools inevitably used various combinations of these approaches, as well as others, in different lessons and to various extremes.

Illustration 3.3: An example of a lesson for an all-girl class

At the same school, Applewood Comprehensive, a Year 11 all-girl, bottom set (n=11), English lesson was observed. The 50-minute lesson was based on a combination of whole-class teaching and individual work.

The girls entered the classroom and sat in rows facing the front of the room. The lesson began with the teacher reading a short poem. The teacher then asked the girls a number of questions about what she had read and wrote their answers on the board; the girls copied them down. She then wrote some more questions and asked the girls to answer following the same structure that they had just used. For the rest of the lesson, the girls were left to work individually, although most of them discussed issues with neighbours. The teacher walked around the class helping those who were 'stuck' and checking that the girls were on-task. In the last few minutes, the teacher wrote the girls' homework on the board and asked them to copy it down.

The lesson was characterised by an air of informality. When the girls were asked questions, they simply answered them by speaking out rather than by putting their hands up and waiting to be asked. However, none of the girls spoke over one another. During the whole-class teaching, the girls sat quietly, whilst during the individual work, there was a constant hum of discussion.

Like the previous illustration, this example highlights some of the typical approaches used by teachers when teaching all-girl classes, such as less structure and more individual/group work. The extent to which teachers used these approaches inevitably varied from teacher to teacher, lesson to lesson and school to school.

Another teaching/classroom management strategy, which was popular among teachers in many of the case study schools, was to introduce an element of competition within the all-boy classes. Teachers felt that this was important because boys tend to find competition enjoyable and motivating. Most of these schools introduced different types of competition based on various football analogies. For example, at one school, boys' marks were used to place them on a league table from which they could be both promoted and relegated, whilst at another school, at the end of each lesson, the boy who had worked the hardest or achieved the most was awarded 'man of the match' status.

Most of the teachers in those schools that had implemented single-sex classes in English also felt that it was important to use materials, especially texts, that were more suitable for the gender of the class that they were teaching. These teachers hoped that by taking this approach, they would be able to generate pupil interest and increase pupils' levels of motivation.

Consequently, within these schools, all-boy classes often studied 'male-oriented' texts (such as *The Lord of the Flies*) while the girls studied 'female-oriented' texts (such as romantic fiction).

In those schools where single-sex classes had been implemented for non-language subjects, such as mathematics and design and technology, staff did not feel that it was necessary to modify curriculum materials for either the boys or the girls. This was because they felt that the single-sex environment and, in the case of mathematics, changes in teaching methods to match the learning styles of boys and girls were sufficient to impact on pupil achievement.

The modification of teaching approaches, in terms of lesson structure, teaching methods and curriculum materials, to match the learning styles of boys and girls can be perceived as an approach that simply reinforces the different learning styles of boys and girls by exploiting the areas where they are strong and by ignoring their areas of weakness. Although this may lead to increased pupil achievement in terms of examination performance, it may have detrimental effects on pupil achievement at a broader level and may work to reinforce gender stereotypes regarding appropriate teaching and learning methods for boys and girls.

Teachers' perceptions of single-sex classes

In the majority of case study schools, teachers were, on the whole, enthusiastic, positive and supportive of the strategy. This appeared to be because they had been involved in the decision to adopt single-sex classes and in review discussions about their impact. In the one case where subject teachers had not been involved in the decision-making process, they expressed a noticeably less enthusiastic response.

At a general level, staff from a number of schools stated that, given their original decision to work in a coeducational school, they preferred teaching mixed-sex classes to single-sex classes. This was on ideological grounds and because they felt that single-sex classes were detrimental to pupils at a social level. However, many teachers appreciated that single-sex classes had the potential to produce academic benefits which could outweigh the social benefits of mixed-gender classes and they therefore considered single-sex classes worth pursuing at an experimental level.

Regardless of these potential benefits, a number of English teachers expressed concern that boys and girls were missing out on one another's approaches to learning, perspectives and opinions. Staff felt that this would have a negative effect on pupils' learning, especially given the importance of debate within the English curriculum. One teacher noted:

> *In English, it is important to get other opinions and interpretations; this is a vital factor that is missing.*

(subject teacher)

However, some of these teachers felt that this limitation was balanced to some extent by the fact that the pupils had the majority of their other subjects in mixed-gender classes and by the conscious attempt of subject teachers to address this issue within lessons.

Staff within the case study schools generally found all-girl classes undemanding in terms of behaviour management and therefore enjoyable to teach. In contrast, regardless of how teachers were allocated to teach single-sex classes, staff in a number of schools expressed concern about having to teach all-boy classes. This was primarily because of the implications for classroom management, as one teacher said:

> *I hadn't realised how locker room it was going to get. I wasn't prepared for the effect of 33 lads with no civilising females.*
>
> (subject teacher)

Staff within two schools where single-sex classes were implemented for pupils of lower ability were specifically concerned about managing the behaviour of low-ability, all-boy classes. One teacher said:

> *You have a concentration of boys of low ability in a relatively large class, which makes it difficult to manage. While all schools have groups like this, the move from coeducational groups to single-sex groups has exacerbated that problem and we haven't got all the solutions for that kind of problem yet.* (subject teacher)

As a result of such concerns in one school, the project coordinator felt that because teachers were asked to volunteer to take single-sex classes, and because many were apprehensive about teaching the all-boy, low-ability class, he found himself having to continually volunteer to take this class. The project coordinator felt that this had led to something of a vicious circle, because whilst his own increased experience enabled him to develop the skills to work effectively with this group of boys, this competence reinforced the apprehension of other staff to volunteer to take the all-boy, low-ability class.

However, at Cherrytree High, where staff were also given the opportunity to volunteer to take single-sex classes, the project coordinator stated that this approach had actually worked in a positive way, because those members of staff who were initially hesitant had the opportunity to learn about teaching single-sex classes from the experiences of colleagues in a way that helped to raise their confidence in teaching those classes.

Teacher – pupil relations

In the majority of schools, staff felt that in order for single-sex classes to work effectively, especially all-boy classes, it was important that there was good rapport between the teacher and the pupils. Schools attempted to facilitate good teacher – pupil relations in two main ways: firstly, by allocating project coordinators to teach the all-boy classes. These teachers were often very well informed, committed and enthusiastic about single-sex classes and consequently their lessons tended to be characterised by the greatest degree of rapport between the teacher and the pupils. One teacher said:

Whether the person taking your boys' group is male or female, you've got to be a strong personality, bossy without being dictatorial. You've got to have a sense of humour, you've got to like boys ... be very fair, take jokes, talk openly about sex and sexism [and you've] *got to have enthusiasm .* (project coordinator)

Secondly, as noted previously, some schools attempted to foster good teacher – pupil relations by allocating male subject teachers to the all-boy classes as they felt that this would help to address the stereotypical perceptions that some boys had about some subjects being 'feminine':

We were very fortunate in having a very positive role model [for the boys] who is very sport-oriented, very masculine and also very literate and intellectual. (subject teacher)

In general, staff perceived that it was important to build up a good rapport with all-boy classes, and therefore made an effort to do so. Unsurprisingly, these lessons were, in the main, well received by the boys. In contrast, staff generally assumed that there was less of a need to consciously build up a good rapport with all-girl classes, possibly because they felt that their relations with female pupils were generally positive anyway.

3.6 Experiences of pupils and parents

This section highlights the experiences of single-sex classes for both pupils and their parents. It begins by outlining the way that staff informed pupils about the strategy. This is followed by a description of the pupils' perceptions and experiences of single-sex classes. The final section describes the involvement and views of parents in relation to their child's involvement in single-sex classes.

The involvement of pupils

In the majority of the schools, staff decided that it was important to involve pupils in the process of implementing single-sex classes. Staff therefore assembled those pupils who would be affected by single-sex classes and told them what they hoped to do and why they were doing it. One teacher said:

I told them we were piloting a new way of teaching which might encourage them to do things they didn't think they could do and to capitalise on the things they could do. (project coordinator)

Staff within these schools noted that it was important for them to present the strategy in a positive light to both the boys and girls who would be involved. However, whilst the staff in some schools felt that it was important not to overstate the use of single-sex classes, in order to avoid any negative reactions from pupils, staff at other schools felt that it was important to be specific so that the targeted pupils appreciated the importance of the strategy and felt a sense of commitment to the project:

> *I was honest with them and said 'You could walk out of the school door in June with one of two results: the pessimistic option, which is one GCSE, and the optimistic, which is nine – they are two different lives: which one do you want?'. They took it seriously ... I was very aware that what I was doing could be counterproductive and I could set up a rebellion ... We didn't do this to the boys, we did it with them. They were part of the strategy.*
>
> (project co-ordinator)

In only one school were pupils given the option of not taking part in the strategy.

Overall, staff stated that they were surprised at how accepting the pupils were of single-sex classes. Few pupils questioned staff about the strategy and only a small number of staff received complaints from pupils, predominantly girls, about being organised into single-sex classes. Some staff did, however, note that a few pupils who had not been targeted for single-sex classes had approached them and asked if they could be involved as they felt that it would help them academically.

Pupils' perceptions and experiences of single-sex classes

Although staff had, in general, tried to present the strategy positively to both boys and girl, the overriding impression of pupils within the schools was that single-sex classes had been implemented primarily in the interests of the boys – as indeed it usually had. For example, some pupils stated that they believed that single-sex classes had been implemented to prevent boys from being distracted by girls.

Previous research which investigated pupils' responses to single-sex classes (Kenway, 1995; Measor *et al.*, 1996; Crump, 1990) found that girls respond more positively to single-sex classes than boys. These researchers suggest that this may be because boys feel they have no one to help them or compete with and are therefore disruptive.

Although the findings from the case study schools in this study contradict these conclusions, they support those of Rowe (1988) by showing that whilst the majority of boys viewed single-sex classes positively, especially in terms of their impact on academic progress, girls tended to hold far more mixed views in terms of both the academic and social impact of these classes. The variation between this finding and previous work in this area can be attributed to the recent emphasis on boys' achievement nationally and the fact that the case study schools in this study implemented single-sex classes primarily to improve boys achievement and used teaching strategies designed to motivate boys.

The findings from the case study schools revealed that single-sex classes were beneficial for boys in four main ways. Firstly, the boys and the teachers interviewed felt that the teaching strategies used within single-sex classes, such as whole-class teaching and lessons which were briskly paced, with a high degree of structured short-term tasks and an element of competition, made lessons more interesting and enjoyable. This increased some boys' levels of motivation and concentration, which impacted positively on the extent to which they remained on-task during lessons and had the added benefit of reducing the incidence of unacceptable behaviour. One teacher noted:

> *Boys who, in other subjects, when they're in different groupings, can be quite some problem, don't seem to be in the all-boys group.*
>
> (project coordinator)

Secondly, the teachers of languages felt, as they had hoped, that the use of male subject teachers as role models helped to challenge boys' stereotypical perceptions of the 'feminine' nature of these subjects and encouraged boys to perceive these subjects as both enjoyable and as areas where they could be successful without losing credibility amongst their peers. One teacher said:

> *I now have a significant group of boys for whom it's OK to like English. There's been a change in the way boys are viewing English.*
>
> (subject teacher)

Thirdly, both the boys and the teachers felt that the all-male environment was more conducive to learning. They claimed that the absence of girls helped to reduce boys' levels of distraction and increased their levels of self-confidence. The boys were therefore more willing to contribute during lessons, arguably because there were no girls to feel inferior to, and more willing to take risks answering questions, possibly because there were no girls to feel embarrassed in front of if the answer was incorrect.

Finally, the boys interviewed felt that single-sex classes had helped to improve their relations with teachers as they believed that in an all-boy class they received more attention during lessons and their achievements were not constantly being overshadowed by the achievements of girls:

> *Last year, boys would never get to be top of the class. It gets you down when you try your hardest; it feels like your teacher doesn't care. In all-boys classes, when you do a good piece of work, the teacher has to notice.*
>
> (Year 8 boy)

Previous research goes some way to supporting this finding, as researchers (Warrington and Younger, 1997; Pickering, 1997) have found that boys in mixed-gender classes tend to feel that they receive less support, encouragement and guidance from their teachers, and that their teachers usually have higher expectations of girls. However, due to the paucity of research in the area of single-sex classes, there is little confirmatory evidence that single-sex classes enable boys to feel more supported and valued by their teachers.

The benefits of single-sex classes for the girls were less apparent to both the girls and their teachers. However, the girls did feel that the absence of boys resulted in fewer classroom distractions, which meant that they received more teacher attention and were better able to concentrate on with their work.

In addition, in a similar way to the boys, both the girls and the teachers interviewed generally felt that single-sex classes helped to increase girls' levels of confidence as the absence of boys meant that they were more prepared to answer questions and were less inhibited in guessing answers:

> *I have found a reduction in the amount of self-consciousness among the girls, particularly when we do group activities where they act out scenes from plays or stories ... they feel less intimidated and more able to speak out.* (subject teacher)

Only a few pupils said that they missed having the opposite sex in class.

Overall, these findings confirm those of Rowe (1988) which examined the effects of single-sex classes on student achievement and confidence in learning mathematics. Through observing classroom interactions, Rowe found that

> *in single-sex classes of either gender there was a notable reduction in the frequency and saliency of student attention-demanding behaviours as well as reduced student discipline and management problems ... such outcomes resulted in perceived increase in both student and teacher 'time on task', impacted positively on teacher expectations of individual student and group performance and encouraged teachers to match both curriculum content and teaching styles to specific gender- and group-related student interests.* (Rowe, 1988, pp. 196-7)

The involvement and views of parents

All but one of the schools felt that it was necessary to inform the parents of targeted pupils that their children were going to be put into single-sex classes. Schools achieved this by sending letters or newsletters out to parents. In general, these letters explained to parents why schools/departments were implementing single-sex classes, offered parents the opportunity to discuss the idea with staff and some asked parents for consent for their child to be placed in a single-sex class.

At one school, letters were only sent to parents once pupils had been informed about the strategy and had agreed to take part. This was done in an attempt to encourage targeted pupils to feel that they had an active and important role in the strategy. In another school, staff felt that it was important for parents to be more involved so they sent out letters to parents at regular intervals informing them of their child's progress and offering parents the opportunity to comment on how well they felt single-sex classes were working for their child (see Appendices 3.1 and 3.2).

Most of the pupils interviewed stated that their parents were aware that they were in single-sex classes. These pupils felt that their parents held a range of views from neutral to positive about the effectiveness of such classes.

In some of the schools, senior members of staff believed that parents generally perceived the use of single-sex classes favourably. One parent, responding to a letter updating her about her son's progress in a single-sex English class, wrote:

Thank you for letting us know how well Stuart is doing in English – with your expert methods, he has never enjoyed English as much.

However, in the majority of schools, because single-sex classes had only recently been introduced, staff felt that they had not had many opportunities (for example, during parents' evenings) to speak to parents about their perceptions of single-sex classes and thus to gain an accurate impression of parents' views.

3.7 The effectiveness of single-sex classes

This section describes the case study schools' evaluation of their use of single-sex classes. It outlines the different types of monitoring systems that schools had in place as well as the findings from schools' evaluations of single-sex classes. This is followed by a summary of the key factors which staff feel are essential for the success of single-sex classes and concludes with suggestions from staff for future changes.

Evidence regarding the success of single-sex classes

In general, staff within most of the schools used a range of both quantitative and qualitative approaches to monitor the impact of single-sex classes. Quantitative methods of monitoring included the analysis of GCSE examination results, test results, the number of pupils taking up particular options and the number of boys and girls being allocated to high sets. In contrast, qualitative methods of monitoring included obtaining feedback through discussions with key participants (such as staff, pupils and parents), obtaining the views of pupils and teachers through questionnaires and assessing pupil behaviour. By taking a two-pronged approach to monitoring, staff within schools were able to gain a holistic view of the impact of the strategy on key participants' experiences of teaching and learning as well as its effect on pupils' levels of achievement.

Schools adopted different forms/combinations of monitoring according to what they hoped to achieve by implementing single-sex classes. For example, the five schools that targeted middle-low-ability pupils in KS4 analysed the success of single-sex classes in terms of GCSE examination results and through informal discussions with staff, pupils and parents. In contrast, the schools targeting Y8 pupils relied on end-of-year tests, changes in pupil behaviour and informal discussions with key participants. Finally, the school which targeted Y9 pupils, in an attempt to increase the number of girls who went on to take design and technology as an option, intended to use female take-up numbers of DT at Y10 as a measure of the success of single-sex classes. The illustration below (3.4) provides a description of the strategy used within one school to monitor and evaluate the impact of single-sex classes.

Illustration 3.4: How one school monitored and evaluated single-sex classes

At Blackberry Hill, staff adopted a two-pronged approach in terms of how they monitored the impact of single-sex classes. At a quantitative level, staff intended to compare pupils' GCSE results with their predicted grades, which were based on KS3 NCAs, for the whole year group and in terms of gender. However, because the first cohort of pupils who had been placed in single-sex classes from the beginning of KS4 were only just coming to the end of Year 11, staff had yet to use this quantitative approach to assess the effectiveness of single-sex classes.

At a qualitative level, however, single-sex classes were also monitored through the use of questionnaires to a sample of pupils (15 pupils from an all-boy class and 15 pupils from an all-girl class) for each year group, at the end of the academic year (see Appendix 3.3 for a copy of the questionnaire and Appendix 3.4 for a copy of the pupils' responses). The strategy was also monitored through information collected from teachers within the English department, who were asked to record their perceptions of the strengths and weaknesses of the strategy (see Appendix 3.5 for a copy of teachers' responses after the first year of the strategy).

Due to the relatively recent introduction of single-sex classes and the impact of continual modifications to the strategy, staff in four of the schools in the study did not feel that it was possible to state, quantitatively, how successful single-sex classes had been. Staff in the remaining schools were able to provide some quantitative evidence, in terms of GCSE examination results, which showed that the boys targeted had done better than teachers had predicted. However, only one school had statistical evidence to show that one cohort of boys in single-sex classes had done significantly better than expected in terms of the target of the strategy – gaining a grade C or above at GCSE.

At a qualitative level, staff in half of the schools stated that, on the basis of intuition and feedback from key participants, they felt that single-sex classes were having a positive effect on pupil achievement for both boys and girls. Their intuition was generally based on factors such as pupils becoming more organised and being up to date with their work. Feedback came from informal discussions with, or questionnaire responses from, staff, pupils and parents (see Appendices 3.4 and 3.5 for examples of feedback comments from pupils and staff at one school).

Staff in a number of schools noted that because single-sex classes were generally having a positive impact on both boys and girls, it was not necessarily helping to reduce the gender gap but simply to maintain it at a higher level of achievement.

This was an interesting finding because schools had generally implemented single-sex classes to improve the achievement of boys and therefore concentrated on modifying their teaching techniques in order to maximise the effect of single-sex classes on boys. In contrast, little attention was paid to the impact of single-sex classes on girls and few modifications were made by teachers to their teaching approaches (primarily because it was felt that 'traditional' approaches were working well as girls were generally outperforming boys).

Staff in a number of the case study schools expressed concern over whether it would ever be possible to assess accurately the impact of single-sex classes, due to the wealth of uncontrollable factors which influence pupil achievement:

> *It is difficult to assess the effectiveness of the single-sex grouping because there are so many changes ... We cannot attribute any rise in achievement purely to the fact that we separated the boys from the girls ... we may have achieved the same results had the classes remained mixed.* (subject teacher)

This confirms the findings of previous studies in which researchers (Daly, 1996; OFSTED and EOC, 1996; Arnot *et al.*, 1998), like the staff quoted above, have argued that the lack of conclusive results regarding the effect of single-sex classes on pupil achievement can be attributed to the scarcity of studies with adequate controls (Daly, 1996) and to the numerous variables that are affected by these forms of organisation (OFSTED and EOC, 1996):

> *It is not easy, for a number of reasons, to assess the impact of single-sex groupings on achievement. The experimental period may be short (and it takes time before the potential benefits of single-sex groupings are discernible in academic performance), and/or other variables may obscure the neatness of the experimental situation.* (Arnot et al., 1998, p. 83)

The future

Staff at all of the schools in the study stated that they intended to continue using single-sex classes in the coming year. However, this was usually dependent on the findings from their end-of-year evaluation of the strategy – in terms of test results and discussions with staff and pupils.

Some teachers said that they would consider modifying their use of single-sex classes in a variety of different ways, such as by:

♦ expanding the approach to the whole year group or to other subject areas;

♦ rotating staff so that they taught both single-sex classes;

♦ improving their systems of monitoring and evaluation by becoming more consistent and rigorous; and

♦ providing staff with further training.

3.8 Summary

This section summarises the main findings from the chapter, highlighting the key factors which appeared to be necessary for the success of single-sex classes and the primary implications of these factors for teaching and learning. For an overview of how single-sex classes were implemented and used within one of the case study schools, see Appendix 3.6.

Rationale for adopting single-sex classes

♦ Staff were usually motivated to investigate the extent of gender differences in performance because of national interest and concern regarding the issue. They typically used statistical information to identify gender gaps in performance and conducted research to establish possible strategies for addressing the issue. Single-sex classes were generally adopted because staff felt that they enabled them to tailor lessons to match the distinct learning styles of boys and girls. Teachers believed that this would help them to challenge pupils' attitudes towards 'non-traditional' subjects, counter anti-learning subcultures (which were prevalent amongst some boys) and thus impact positively on pupil achievement and gender gaps in performance.

Implementing single-sex classes

♦ For single-sex classes to be implemented efficiently and effectively, it was important that staff perceived the use of single-sex classes in experimental terms, as a possible strategy to adopt, monitor and modify according to its impact and the changing needs of pupils and staff. It was also essential that all staff within the department were included in all aspects of the decision-making process, in terms of whether to adopt single-sex classes, which pupils to target, how to provide staff with the training and support that they needed and how to allocate staff to teach single-sex classes. Finally, the findings from the case study schools indicate that although schools had identified, at a general level, where gender differences in achievement were prevalent, it was important that single-sex classes were targeted at a specific group of pupils, in terms of subject area, year group and ability level, which directly impacted on where the gender gap in performance lay.

♦ In general, few practical preparations had to be made and schools required little funding to implement single-sex classes. Staff at some schools had felt it necessary to purchase some resources (primarily books which targeted boys) but the costs for these were usually incurred within departmental budgets. Staff used a variety of quantitative and qualitative methods to identify which pupils would be placed into single-sex classes.

Teaching single-sex classes

♦ To capitalise on the use of single-sex classes, it was important that teachers were aware of the main issues regarding gender differences in performance and appreciated the need to modify their teaching approaches to cater effectively for the different learning styles of boys and girls.

♦ In general, teachers changed their approach to teaching all-boy classes according to evidence from research in this area, by modifying lesson structures, teaching methods and curriculum materials. Attempts were made to build up rapport between teachers and the boys in the all-boy classes by allocating staff who were comprehensively aware of the issues related to gender gaps in performance and by allocating male teachers to all-boy classes. In contrast, teachers did not tend to modify their teaching approaches to cater for the learning styles of girls, possibly because they felt that current approaches were working effectively as the girls were, in general, outperforming the boys.

♦ Teachers generally perceived all-girl classes to be easier and more enjoyable to teach, as all-boy classes, especially those of low ability, required careful behaviour management. There was some concern by teachers that single-sex classes prevented pupils from obtaining the perspective of the opposite sex, which they felt limited pupils' understanding, especially in English lessons.

Pupils' experiences of single-sex classes

♦ It was considered important that pupils were informed about the strategy and that the strategy was presented to them in a positive light. However, given that the focus was primarily on boys, it was unsurprising that pupils generally perceived that single-sex classes had been implemented in the interest of boys and that boys tended to hold more positive perceptions of single-sex classes than girls.

♦ Boys benefited from single-sex classes because: the changes in teaching approaches increased their levels of interest and motivation; the absence of girls helped to improve their confidence, their level of involvement in lessons and their relations with teachers (in terms of the amount of attention that they received); and having male teachers as role models challenged their stereotypical perceptions of the 'femininity' of certain subjects and the anti-learning culture that some staff felt was prevalent amongst some groups of boys.

♦ The benefits for the girls were less obvious but it was felt that the absence of the boys led to greater teacher attention, fewer distractions and an increase in their level of confidence.

Evaluating single-sex classes

♦ In order to gain an accurate insight into the effect of single-sex classes on both pupil achievement and the lived experiences of teachers, boys and girls, it seemed important to use a combination of both quantitative and qualitative methods to monitor single-sex classes. However, there was a general appreciation that it was difficult to assess accurately the impact of single-sex classes due to their relatively recent introduction within most schools and the numerous, uncontrollable factors which could also impinge upon pupil performance.

♦ At the time of this study, few schools had quantitative evidence to support the use of single-sex classes. However, those which did revealed that single-sex classes were having an initial, positive impact on pupil achievement. The findings from qualitative forms of evaluations, such as feedback from key participants, appeared to support this initial finding. Although these initial, tentative assessments suggested that single-sex classes were having a positive effect on pupil achievement, they also revealed that these classes were not necessarily helping to reduce the gender gap as girls were benefiting as much as boys from being put into single-sex classes.

In brief, the following list highlights the factors which staff felt were important for ensuring that single-sex classes were implemented effectively and efficiently.

KEY FACTORS THAT MAKE THE SINGLE-SEX CLASSES WORK

- **a school ethos that encourages experimentation with different strategies, enabling staff to modify and expand their approaches;**

- **staff who are not only capable of implementing the strategy but who support the theory behind single-sex classes and are therefore willing to modify their teaching approaches accordingly;**

- **the allocation of members of staff to the all-boy (especially) and all-girl class who will be able to build up the rapport needed to help ensure that single-sex classes are productive;**

- **presenting the strategy positively to pupils.**

4. MENTORING

4.1 Setting the context

One suggested way of addressing the gender gap in performance is to provide mentors for pupils, in an attempt to tackle factors which may be preventing them from fulfilling their potential. This chapter begins by providing an overview of the main issues regarding mentoring.

Mentoring has its origins in the United States and has traditionally been used in the world of industry and commerce (Kerry, 1998; McNally, 1994). However, in recent years, it has become increasingly popular in Britain and is used in a wide variety of situations. For example, although it continues to be used within business, it is also increasingly used in adult education, initial teacher training, higher education and secondary education (Hirom and Mitchell, 1999; Golden and Sims, 1997; Merriam, 1983; Kerry, 1998). Within secondary schools, it has been found that mentoring is primarily used as a supplement to the traditional work of the tutor (Hylan and Postlethwaite, 1997; Gay, 1994), although it can take the form of anything from tutoring to counselling (Hirom and Mitchell, 1999). It also represents a major element in the application and delivery of Compact agreements for school pupils.

Commentators within the field (McNally, 1994; Merriam, 1983; Woodd, 1997) have noted that mentoring can be defined in a number of ways as it can mean different things in different settings. The word 'mentor' comes from Greek mythology, when Ulysses entrusted his son to the care of his friend, Mentor (Clutterbuck, 1991). This portrays the image of a senior or older person watching over a younger person and acting as an adviser and guide.

Gay (1994) has suggested that mentoring in education can most appropriately be defined as a supportive relationship between a youth and someone who offers support, guidance and concrete assistance, as the younger partner goes through a difficult period. Thus the role of the mentor encapsulates that of teacher, counsellor, negotiator, supervisor, entertainer and coach.

Similarly, Beattie and Holden (1994) have revealed that the mentoring of a young person can include a variety of relationships such as:

- *A one-to-one relationship, over a period of time, between a young person and an adult, which provides consistent support, guidance and practical help as the young person goes through a difficult or challenging period of life.*

- *The process by which an adult shares his/her personal knowledge, skills and experience with a young person.*

- *An opportunity for a young person to access impartial, non-judgmental adult advice and support.*

- *A two-way process in which both mentors and young people derive satisfaction from their alliance* (pp. 8-9).

Beattie and Holden (1994) have also suggested that the mentor – pupil relationship progresses through three phases – from a general sharing of information, to the exploring and clarifying of thoughts and feelings, and finally to the planning and setting of objectives that will enable support. The researchers note that the rate of progress depends on the relationship between the individuals involved.

A number of recent studies (Hirom and Mitchell, 1999; Hylan and Postlethwaite, 1997; Golden and Sims, 1997; Beattie and Holden, 1994) have been conducted into the use of both internal and industrial mentoring within secondary schools. These studies suggest that mentoring is often perceived as a way to improve pupil self-esteem, to fulfil the potential of pupils and to address any additional needs that they might have. It is therefore frequently used to address underachievement among pupils and to prepare them for the world of work.

This chapter builds on this research by investigating the way in which eight secondary schools used mentoring to help pupils fulfil their potential and thereby contributed to addressing gender differences in achievement. The chapter will present:

♦ the rationale behind teachers' adoption of mentoring;

♦ descriptions of the different mentoring schemes used and how they were implemented; and

♦ an assessment of the impact that mentoring had on key participants.

4.2 Rationale for implementing mentoring schemes

As in the schools which had adopted single-sex classes, interviews with staff from the eight case study schools revealed that gender differences in achievement had been identified through statistical analyses of school tests, investigations into pupil participation in school activities and a general recognition that some groups of pupils were underachieving. Within the case study schools, the majority of these pupils were boys. There was also a general awareness among staff that boys' levels of achievement, in comparison to girls, were of national interest and concern. One teacher said:

The picture throughout this analysis was that girls were not only achieving at a higher level they were also more active and they were actually gaining more from school life. (project coordinator)

Why adopt mentoring?

Previous research (Hylan and Postlethwaite, 1997; Golden and Sims, 1997; Beattie and Holden, 1994) has suggested that mentoring can be used to tackle the issue of underachievement and, in general, staff within the case study schools supported this view. They held clear conceptions of why they believed mentoring would enable them to tackle gender differences in achievement.

To begin with, staff across all eight schools felt that mentoring allowed them to target specific groups of pupils (usually underachieving boys) with particular forms of support which catered for their needs. For example, research has shown that boys and girls interact with curriculum content differently and favour different styles of response, reflecting often gendered reading and writing preferences (Bleach, 1998b; Murphy and Elwood, 1996; OFSTED and EOC, 1996; Arnot *et al.*, 1998). It is therefore important that the learning styles of boys and girls are developed so that they are provided with the opportunity to appreciate the value of different ways of working and communicating for different purposes (Murphy and Elwood, 1998). Reflecting these findings, staff at the case study schools felt that mentoring would enable them to help targeted pupils address their weaknesses and thus improve their learning skills. For boys, this often meant focusing on issues of organisation, time management, revision and literacy skills whilst for girls this usually meant focusing on coping with pressure, writing succinctly and targeting specific areas of weakness in a variety of subject areas.

Secondly, research (Bray *et al.*, 1997; Pickering, 1997; Gallagher, 1997; Cohen, 1998) suggests that, in general, there is an anti-schooling/anti-learning subculture among some boys. It has been argued that this derives from the lack of contact that many boys have with male role models during their schooling careers, which combines with their development (where boys take on a desire to be as unfeminine as possible) to lead some boys to perceive schooling and learning as effeminate. This then encourages some boys to develop negative attitudes towards schooling and learning. Reflecting an appreciation of this argument, staff within the case study schools hoped that mentoring would also help to improve pupils' confidence, attitudes and motivation towards schooling and learning, thereby addressing the anti-learning subculture that was prevalent among some groups of boys. Staff hoped this would impact positively on pupil achievement across the curriculum and thus overall gender differences in performance:

> *The main aims are to raise pupils' confidence, expectations and self-esteem. To review and improve, where necessary, attendance and punctuality. To look at pupils' academic progress and encourage them to monitor their own progress and identify their own strengths and weaknesses. And also to help pupils set targets and action-plans that will lead, we hope, to improved GCSEs.*
>
> (school policy document on mentoring)

Staff at two schools where Year 8 pupils were targeted agreed with these aims for mentoring but adopted a more subject-focused approach. Their main reason for developing mentoring schemes was to help (predominantly male) pupils improve their levels of literacy, which, staff felt, would impact on pupil achievement, reducing gender gaps in performance. One school therefore decided to implement a paired reading scheme where Year 8 pupils were paired with Year 12 students, while the other decided to run an after-school, all-boy, literacy club. Staff at both of these schools hoped that these strategies would enhance these boys' attitudes and improve their levels of confidence, motivation and ability in literacy.

The specific incentives which led staff within schools to adopt mentoring came from a variety of sources. These included previous experience of using mentoring schemes during LEA-based projects on raising achievement, prior experience of implementing mentoring schemes when at other schools, brainstorming sessions with other members of staff, and reading-related literature.

For example, staff at two of the schools had previously taken part in 'Raising Achievement Projects' initiated by their LEA. Although the focus of these projects varied (one focused on underachieving *pupils*, while the other focused on underachieving *boys*), staff at both of these schools had decided to adopt some form of mentoring as one of a number of strategies for dealing with the issue under investigation. Due to the success of the schemes, staff decided to continue their use of mentoring in an attempt to address gender differences in achievement once these projects had finished.

What schools hoped to achieve

In general, staff within the eight case study schools stated that their overall target was to simultaneously address gender differences in performance and overall levels of achievement.

4.3 Mentoring programmes

This section describes the different types of mentoring schemes that were adopted and implemented within the eight case study schools. It outlines which pupils were targeted, how the programmes were organised and the general structure of mentoring sessions.

Pupils targeted

Research indicates that mentoring schemes within secondary schools often target specific groups of pupils (Hylan and Postlethwaite, 1997). Golden and Sims (1997) noted that the majority of the 94 industrial mentoring schemes in their study targeted pupils in Years 10 and 11. In particular, 81 per cent of the schemes targeted specific groups of pupils, primarily underachievers, but also pupils with special educational needs, pupils from particular ethnic minority backgrounds and pupils of a particular gender. Reflecting these findings, six of the case study schools in this study implemented mentoring schemes to target pupils in KS4. Of these, four targeted pupils in Year 11, one targeted all pupils in KS4 and one targeted Year 10 pupils. The remaining two case study schools targeted pupils in Year 8. Table 4.1 below provides an overview of the different pupils targeted by the case study schools.

Table 4.1: The different pupils targeted by the mentoring schemes

School	Year	Pupils targeted	Process of identification	No. of pupils	Subjects targeted
Abbott High	Y11	Pupils on the 5+ A-C border All interested pupils	KS3 results school reports Y10 results	20	Cross-curricular
Bacon Comp.	Y11	Pupils on the 5+ A-C border All interested pupils	YELLIS scores, teacher assessments	32	Cross-curricular
Constable Lane	Y11	Pupils on the 5+ A-C border Pupils who are 'more able'	KS3 results,, NFER tests, Mock exam results	53 43	Cross-curricular
Dobson Road	Y11	Pupils on the 5+ A-C border	YELLIS, Year 10 and 11 tests	30	Cross-curricular
Epstein Sec.	Y10	All pupils	N/A	221	Cross-curricular
Flaxman Comp.	Y11 & Y10	Pupils underachieving (regardless of ability)	Y7 CAT scores, KS3 results GCSE predictions	30	Cross-curricular
Gainsborough High	Y8	Pupils underachieving in literacy	Y7 reading tests, teacher assessments	16	English – reading
Hogarth Comp.	Y8	Pupils underachieving	English set place, projected GCSE grade in English	15-20 15-20	English English

As the table shows, of the six schools that targeted KS4 pupils, four focused on those pupils who were on the five or more A – C GCSE borderline, the majority of whom were boys. Staff felt that by providing support for these borderline pupils they would be able to improve levels of achievement, effectively and efficiently, both for these pupils and other pupils within the school. Many teachers believed that this was because borderline pupils only needed support at a relatively superficial level in order to make a significant impact on their levels of achievement in terms of the current criteria (i.e. five or more C+ at GCSE). In addition, some teachers claimed that once these pupils began to achieve, this would have a 'knock-on' effect on other pupils, which would improve the achievement ethos of the school. It was also felt that because the majority of these pupils were boys, it would allow schools to close any gender gap in performance that was currently existing:

The crunch lies with the boys and girls at the five A – C borderline. That is where things can be improved dramatically. You don't need innate skill to improve here just – organisation and motivation.

(headteacher)

Interestingly, staff at some schools explicitly stated that the main reason for addressing borderline pupils was external pressures. One teacher stated that because schools are under increasing pressure to improve examination results there is a strong incentive for staff to focus on pupils who are on the five or more A – C GCSE borderline as this is the main criterion upon which schools are judged. The teacher stated that whilst these pupils may be in need of support to ensure that they fulfil their potential they are not necessarily the pupils who are underachieving to the greatest extent. One project coordinator stated:

One of the obvious outcomes of Government policy which makes schools accountable is that there is going to be a concentration around those kids who are at the margins or borders of the criteria you are assessing.

To some extent, this substantiates the suggestion made by Mahony (1998), who argued that the move towards a market-led education system has increased the focus on pupil attainment and consequently the pressure on schools to identify ways of supporting pupils who underachieve according to this criterion (such as boys), as the performance of these pupils is crucial in determining the overall performance of schools.

However, staff within many of the schools explained that although they were focusing on borderline pupils, they were not succumbing to national concerns by concentrating only on boys, as this did not provide equality of opportunity. Furthermore, they did not want to raise the achievement of boys at the expense of girls:

There were some students [girls] in the middle band of the year group, in terms of ability, who, like the boys, could slip through the net and not achieve to their potential. (project coordinator)

In addition, staff in a number of schools stated that as well as targeting pupils who were at the academic borderline, they also targeted other pupils who they thought would benefit from being mentored. For example, staff at two schools noted that instead of just targeting pupils who were underachieving academically, they also targeted pupils who were perceived to be underachieving socially. Secondly, staff at Constable Lane noted that they also targeted 'more able' boys as the girls of high ability were achieving more A*s – As at GCSE than the boys of high ability. Finally, staff at Abbott High and Bacon Comprehensive revealed that in order to ensure equality of opportunity, they opened their mentoring programme up to all non-targeted pupils in the year who expressed an interest in taking part. Taking the concept of equality of opportunity further, staff at Epstein Secondary decided that all pupils in the target year group (Y10) would take part in the programme as the headteacher felt that

> *to maximise the potential of everyone I would say that every child should be mentored ... it is a case of easing out the issues for the child and seeing what the child wants or needs from the sessions irrespective of their gender.* (headteacher)

In order to identify the target pupils, all of these schools used a wide range of sources, such as statistical data on pupil performance over a number of years (KS3 tests, YELLIS tests, Y10 examination results) and teacher assessments and examination predictions:

> *So the initial grouping (for participation in the mentoring programme) in year ten is based almost entirely on data that we have from Years 7, 8 and 9.* (headteacher)

Illustration 4.1: How target pupils were identified at one school

At Constable Lane, the identification of boys on the borderline of five or more A – Cs at GCSE for participation in the school's mentoring programme became more precise as time went on. The project coordinator noted that for the pilot of the programme, staff simply looked at the predicted grades taken from the Year 11 mock examination results in January and targeted those boys who were expected to obtain three or four A – C grades at GCSE. However, in the second year, staff took a slightly more sophisticated approach. Teachers were asked to predict pupils' final grades prior to their mocks and those boys who were predicted three or four A – C grades were targeted. This enabled the mentoring programme to start more promptly after the Christmas break. In addition, staff looked at pupils' results from their KS3 NCA tests to identify those who were on target, at the end of Year 9, to achieve five or more A – C grades at GCSE, and investigated whether these pupils were predicted to fulfil that expectation by their teachers in Year 11. If they were not, these pupils were also targeted. The project coordinator noted that in the coming year, staff were considering using NFER reading tests to identify underachieving borderline pupils rather than KS3 NCA tests as staff held some reservations about the reliability of NCA tests.

As mentioned previously, Gainsborough High and Hogarth Comprehensive focused on pupils in Year 8 because they wanted to address underachievement in literacy. Again, the majority of these pupils tended to be boys. In general, staff had decided to implement their mentoring programmes to target Year 8 pupils because this appeared to be when many boys developed negative perceptions and attitudes towards literacy. Staff hoped that by tackling the issue at this level, they would be able to prevent boys from developing a negative orientation towards literacy which would impact positively on their levels of achievement and enable them to access a wider range of texts both within English and across the curriculum:

> *It seemed to me to indicate that Year 8 was the year when, in secondary schools, very many boys stop reading altogether.* (project coordinator)

Staff at these two schools also identified pupils who were underachieving in terms of literacy skills through a variety of tests (e.g. KS2 NCA tests, reading tests) and teacher assessments:

So anyone who had a reading age of three years or less [than their chronological age] *was automatically selected and then the others were children who I knew were having difficulties with their reading generally ... two of those students actually have very low self-esteem and don't have a lot of confidence, so a bit of judgement was also used.* (project coordinator)

Structure of programmes

The mentoring programmes varied in terms of how they were organised. Table 4.2 summarises the main characteristics of each of the schemes adopted by the eight case study schools.

Table 4.2: The characteristics of the different mentoring schemes.

School	Duration of programme	Frequency of session	Length of sessions	Place of sessions	Key participants
Abbott High	Throughout Y11	Negotiable	Negotiable	Out of lessons	Staff mentor one-to-one
Bacon Comp.	Throughout Y11	Once a fortnight	15-30 mins	Out of lessons	Staff mentor one-to-one
Constable Lane	Jan. – end of Y11	Once a fortnight	30 mins	Out of lessons	Staff mentor small groups of pupils
Dobson Road	Jan. – end of Y11	Once a week	15 mins	Out of lessons	Staff mentor one-to-one
Epstein Sec.	Throughout Y10	Once a term	15 mins	During lessons	Form tutor mentors one-to-one
Flaxman Comp.	Throughout KS4	Once a term	20 mins	During lessons	Staff mentor possibly with local employer and parent.
Gainsborough High	From Y8 ongoing	Three times a week	20 mins	Out of lessons	Year 12 student paired with Y8 pupil, one-to-one
Hogarth Comp.	Throughout Y8	Once a week	One hour	Out of lessons	Teacher takes class after school

The mentoring programmes within the schools had been in place for different periods of time ranging from 1995 to 1998. Of the six schools that targeted pupils at KS4, the schemes varied in terms of their duration. Some schools ran the programme throughout the final year, others from January to May of Year 11 and some whenever staff felt pupils were in need of it. The project coordinator at one school noted:

If it's perceived that their performance has gone up and they are able to sustain their own performance then they will come off, and by the same system anyone who's not being seen to be able to sustain performance will come on. (project coordinator)

The mentoring sessions at these schools also varied in frequency from once a week to once a term. At Abbott High, mentors and pupils were able to negotiate how often they had sessions. The length of sessions tended to range from 15 – 30 minutes across all schools:

Sessions can last up to half an hour ... most see their mentor after school. We don't mind seeing them for half an hour because we need their help with revision ... if the mentor is prepared to put their effort in, then I think we should be too. (Year 11 girl)

In four of these schools, sessions took place out of lesson time while the remaining two schools arranged for mentoring sessions to be incorporated in the timetable. In contrast to this general policy, following an investigation into the impact of mentoring on the achievement of boys, Hirom and Mitchell (1999) suggested that it was important for mentoring sessions to be scheduled during lesson time so that pupils did not regard them as a punishment. However, this did not appear to be a problem within the case study schools.

Research in this area (Golden and Sims, 1997; Beattie and Holden, 1994), has shown that mentoring is most commonly done on a one-to-one basis. Such research suggests that the main advantage of this approach is that it allows personal relationships to develop, without having to account for the effects of peer pressure, and it facilitates the management and coordination of out-of-school mentors (Golden and Sims, 1997). There is some debate about whether group mentoring can actually be said to be 'mentoring' as it does not incorporate primary characteristics such as confidentiality and the opportunity to receive undivided attention. Nevertheless, it has been noted (Golden and Sims, 1997; Beattie and Holden, 1994) that group mentoring does have added advantages such as enabling a greater number of pupils to participate in schemes and the opportunity for fostering peer support.

In general, members of staff at the case study schools mentored pupils on a one-to-one basis. At Constable Lane, pupils were mentored by staff in small groups whilst at Flaxman Comprehensive pupils, where possible, were also allocated a local employer mentor.

The two case study schools which targeted pupils in Year 8 implemented programmes designed explicitly to improve pupils' levels of achievement. Gainsborough High implemented a paired reading scheme between Y8 and Y12 pupils, which took place three times a week for 20 minutes in place of assembly on a one-to-one basis. Hogarth Comprehensive targeted Year 8 boys and decided to implement a weekly after-school lesson that lasted for an hour.

Structure of sessions

A study by Hylan and Postlethwaite (1997) of internal mentoring at a comprehensive girls' school provides a useful, general description of the structure of typical mentoring sessions. They note that the girls were allocated staff mentors who were not their tutors and meetings were held twice a term for 15 minutes. During the meetings, the mentors and the students agreed targets and the mentors suggested practical ways in which the targets might be achieved. The girls' progress on the targets was discussed at the start of the following meeting and both parties kept a record of the discussion.

Although the mentoring schemes developed within the case study schools were quite diverse, the sessions all tended to follow a similar general structure to that outlined above. For example, mentors and pupils often used sessions to work collaboratively to review the extent to which pupils had managed to achieve targets agreed at a previous session. Staff and pupils then usually discussed how well the pupils felt they were doing and any problems that they were experiencing, often in relation to their Records of Achievement. They then identified possible targets for the following period and discussed strategies by which to attain them (see Appendix 4.1). A record of each session was usually kept (see Appendix 4.2) and the mentors often sent memos to relevant teachers informing them whom they were mentoring, asking subject teachers to keep them informed about the progress of the pupils being mentored and letting subject teachers know about any targets that had been set which related to their subject area (see Appendix 4.3).

The targets set covered a wide range of different areas such as attendance, punctuality, behaviour, personal organisation, deadlines for the completion of coursework and homework, time management, revision plans and gathering information on future career plans. Staff at a number of schools also noted that targets were often set to address the different weaknesses that boys and girls have in terms of their learning style:

> *Mentors are aware of gender differences and in their sessions will look at ways boys and girls work ... with girls they do what we call 'busy work', where they spend hours writing out notes and writing them out again and again without reviewing them. Boys on the other hand, tend to do things by shorthand and once they've done it, quickly, they don't really analyse what they've done.*
>
> (headteacher)

The illustrations below provide examples of mentoring sessions held for a male and a female pupil.

Illustration 4.2:   An example of a mentoring session for a male pupil

A one-to-one mentoring session was observed at Abbott High between a staff mentor and a Year 11 male pupil. The session lasted for about 15 minutes and took place in the school's conference room.

The pupil entered the room and after a brief greeting, the mentor presented the pupil with his 'Record Sheet'. Together they went through the sheet discussing the pupil's study skills and homework habits. They then talked about the boy's achievements in particular subject areas. Although the conversation was directed by the mentor, the pupil took an active role, responding openly to questions asked and identifying the root of problems for himself, such as his tendency to be easily distracted. The mentor made a specific effort to highlight the positive comments that had been made and told the pupil that his mock results showed an encouraging development. This pleased both the mentor and the pupil. There was also a brief discussion about the pupil's out-of-school activities.

In the final few minutes, the mentor reviewed what they had discussed and together they identified targets for the pupil to concentrate on. These included obtaining further support in science-based subjects and getting late coursework completed.

Illustration 4.3:   An example of a mentoring session for a female pupil

A one-to-one mentoring session was observed at Abbott High between a staff mentor and a Year 11 female pupil. The session lasted for about 15 minutes and took place in the school's conference room.

The pupil entered the room and after a brief greeting, the mentor and pupil began to go through the pupil's 'Record Sheet', which highlighted her study habits. They then used the pupil's study diary, which she had been asked to keep at the last session, to discuss her progress in individual subject areas. Although the mentor directed the discussion, the pupil participated fully, helping to identify areas of difficulty and to suggest possible solutions to address them. For example, the pupil stated that her workload was causing her to feel under stress so the mentor offered to set up a meeting where they could discuss ways of coping with exam- and work-related stress. In addition, the pupil stated that she felt that her mock examination grades were inaccurate, so the mentor agreed to check them out for her by the next session.

At the end of the meeting, the mentor reviewed and summarised the targets set during the session and asked the pupil whether she agreed with the summary.

4.4   The process of implementation

This section highlights the process that staff at the eight case study schools went through in order to implement their mentoring programmes. It outlines the practical preparations that were made, the training that was provided for mentors and how the programmes were funded. Finally, it presents the difficulties that staff experienced and the consequent modifications that they made to their programmes.

Practical preparations

The only school that had to rearrange its timetable to accommodate the mentoring programme was Epstein Secondary, which targeted all Year 10 pupils. In its scheme, one hour each fortnight was set aside so that form tutors could mentor four of their Year 10 tutees during lesson time.

Gainsborough High solved the problem of finding a time for the mentoring programme by running it during assembly. This time was chosen so that pupils did not miss out on lesson time and it provided the scheme with status as assembly was compulsory for all pupils and staff. However, this created its own difficulties, as the headteacher was not happy that pupils were missing assembly because, as a Church School, this time was used for worship. This school also had to obtain new resources: books which it was hoped would appeal to boys and other reluctant readers.

Training for mentors

Previous research (Golden and Sims, 1997; Beattie and Holden, 1994; Kerry, 1998; Hirom and Mitchell, 1999) has shown that it is essential for schemes to offer training to mentors so that they know what their role entails and are therefore able to carry it out successfully. Golden and Sims (1997) note that all of the 94 industrial schemes in their study offered mentors some form of training which, with hindsight, most mentors valued. In addition, Beattie and Holden (1994) found that, in general, mentors found training useful in terms of providing a framework for action, as a form of support and for ensuring consistency of approach.

Seven of the eight case study schools provided staff mentors with training. The training provided ranged from formal to informal and changed as the scheme became more embedded within the culture of the school. When schemes were initially implemented, the project coordinators at three of the schools went on a number of courses on mentoring and gender differences in achievement. They cascaded information back to staff during INSET sessions on an informal basis. One school reinforced this information by providing a number of half-day training sessions. At three schools, an educational consultant/trainer was invited in to provide mentors, and in one case all staff, with training. At a further two schools, the members of staff with relevant experience provided mentors with training over a number of hourly sessions.

Three of the schools also provided mentors with a set of guidelines (see Appendix 4.4) and additional information such as what the main aims of the scheme were, an outline of the role of mentors and pupils, and strategies for fulfilling responsibilities (see Appendix 4.5). Mentors in three of the schools also mentioned that they received advice, generally from project coordinators or other mentors, on an informal basis:

> *We got little booklets from when it was National Reading Year and booklets on things to pick up on when they were struggling and that. It was quite helpful.* (Year 12 mentor)

At half of these schools, regardless of how comprehensive staff training schemes were, staff stated that they would have preferred further or ongoing training in order to be properly equipped to mentor effectively. Staff at one school would also have liked greater involvement in how the programme was structured, whilst at another school, some staff claimed that they believed the lack of appropriate training led some colleagues to decide against volunteering to become staff mentors.

Funding

At five schools, small amounts of funding were made available through the school budget or departmental budgets to cover administration costs. One of these schools also received money from the LEA to pay for an educational consultant to train staff. Another received additional funding from a number of 'National Year of Reading' schemes to pay for new resources.

Constable Lane received £4,000 from the school budget to cover project management, staff time and the prizes that were required for their mentoring programme. Epstein Secondary and Flaxman Comprehensive received notable amounts of funding from their local Training and Enterprise Councils to implement their mentoring programmes. The funding paid for the management of the project, cover (so that staff could be withdrawn from classes to mentor pupils) and the paperwork required for the project.

Difficulties and modifications

Many of the schools experienced practical difficulties with the implementation of their schemes. Some experienced time constraints, in terms of finding a suitable opportunity to train all mentors, finding a time to run the programme and deciding on the length of sessions. A number of schools found the administration for the programmes complicated and time-consuming and one school found it difficult to organise the programme so that both mentors and pupils had some choice in whom they were paired with. However, two schools did not experience any problems with implementing their programmes.

As a result of difficulties experienced with implementation some schools modified their programmes. Staff at five of the schools noted that, following the pilot of their programmes, the following changes were made: more detailed guidelines for staff were developed; the identification of target pupils was either instigated or refined; pupils (in some schools) were allowed to take part in the process of mentor selection; the number of pupils participating increased; paperwork improved; and the sessions were structured in more detail.

Staff at some schools also stated that in the pilot year, they had used local employers as mentors as well as staff. The project coordinators at these schools felt that the local employers brought an important angle to the sessions for two main reasons. Firstly, it was felt that local employers could speak authoritatively about the world of work and the relationship between employment and education in a way that had a powerful influence on pupils. Secondly, staff noted that the use of local employers provided them with an additional opportunity to expose their (male) pupils to a positive male role model, a factor which some staff felt was lacking within the school environment.

However, after the first year of the mentoring schemes, these schools all but stopped using employer mentors because they found it difficult to sustain recruitment and organise sessions. A headteacher at one school commented:

> *Because of changes in personnel in organisations, and because of pressures in people's work environments, the support we've had more recently from the employers has fallen off; in fact we've only got one person who tends to come on a regular basis.*

This confirms the findings of Golden and Sims (1997), whose study on industrial mentoring revealed that some staff experienced difficulties in the recruitment and retention of out-of-school mentors because of time constraints and changes in the job description of employer mentors.

One of the case study schools focusing on improving the literacy levels of Year 8 pupils simply changed the focus of the programme from writing to reading after a year. At two schools, no changes were made because the programmes had only recently been implemented.

4.5 The mentor's experience

This section describes the mentors' experience across the eight case study schools in terms of their role and how they were recruited, their perceptions of their mentoring programmes and how they were paired with pupils.

The role and recruitment of mentors

The role of the mentor was perceived as roughly similar across all schools. Dobson Road School's policy document summarised this role by stating that the job of the mentor is:

1. to act as a 'critical friend' by helping the student to review and plan their progress;

2. to discuss the work of the individual concerned and identify appropriate strategies and targets;

3. to liaise closely with parents to reinforce success and build on opportunities which warrant praise;

4. to develop a revision programme and work on revision skills/ techniques with the student.

The document noted that the mentor's role is NOT to impinge on the tutor or subject teacher's role and NOT to act in a disciplinary capacity.

In the six schools that targeted pupils at KS4, the pupils were mentored by staff mentors. In three of these schools, staff were asked to volunteer for the role. A project coordinator at one of these schools stated that staff with relevant experience, such as training in counselling, were particularly targeted and asked to volunteer. It was generally felt that staff within these three schools volunteered because they appreciated the benefits which mentoring could have for pupils. At the other three schools, the responsibility for mentoring was usually assigned to senior members of staff, heads of the relevant years and the form tutors of targeted pupils. In the majority of the schools, staff mentored two to five pupils each year. At Epstein Secondary, form tutors had responsibility for mentoring all pupils in their form once a term as this was the only practical way to provide mentoring to all pupils in the year.

In Gainsborough High, Year 8 pupils were paired with a Y12 student for reading sessions/mentoring. The Y12 students were asked to volunteer to participate in the paired reading scheme. The project coordinator stated that although the Y12 students were not put under any pressure to volunteer, persuasion was used by selling the scheme to them

> *as really good experience in terms of applying to universities, putting it on their UCAS forms ... and ... a way for them to give something back to a school that has supported them for the last five years.* (project coordinator)

Finally, at Hogarth Comprehensive, which also targeted Year 8, the pupils received extra support/mentoring from the project coordinator/English teacher who taught the pupils in an after-school club.

Pairing mentors with pupils

In the majority of schools, once pupils agreed to participate in the programme, they were paired with a mentor. Staff and pupils felt that the pairing process was important because for mentoring to work effectively, mentors and pupils had to get on well. As a result, some staff and pupils felt that they should be given some choice in the person they were paired with. The process by which pupils and mentors were paired up varied from school to school. In most schools, pairs were simply organised randomly or on the basis of practicality. In only one school were staff given the opportunity to say whom they would like to mentor (usually a pupil whom they knew quite well). In two schools, pupils were given the option of having a different mentor if they did not feel that they would be able to build up a productive relationship with the one that they had been allocated.

Mentors' perceptions of mentoring

Staff at three of the schools felt that the implementation of the project had created a lot of extra work for project coordinators. The day-to-day running of the project was not, however, perceived by staff at the majority of the schools as work that was adding significantly to their workload.

Overall, staff were generally supportive of their school's mentoring programmes and in some schools, had become increasingly so as they had witnessed the benefits of the programme for pupils. However, within some schools, staff held mixed opinions. In terms of staff – pupil relations, staff at a number of schools claimed that mentoring had had a positive impact:

> *I feel slightly more pressured, slightly more responsible for their achievements and their overall well- being in school.* (staff mentor)

> *From a professional point of view, it helps me to understand some of the difficulties that pupils have at this very stressful time in their school careers.* (staff mentor)

Time, was an issue for staff at all case study schools. At one school, some staff felt that although their mentoring sessions were timetabled into their work schedules, this was not sufficient given the extra work which was required. Staff at other schools felt that because of time constraints, mentors did not receive enough support to fulfil their role and that there was not enough time to monitor what mentors were doing. This often meant that pupils were receiving different levels of mentoring and that there was a lack of communication between key participants:

> *I don't think we're giving enough support to the mentors ... it's hard to give everybody as much feedback, information, help, suggestions as you should.* (staff mentor)

Other limitations that arose at different schools included: the fact that mentoring was done by mentors on a voluntary basis and therefore without pay; the demands of programmes in terms of labour; and the controversy surrounding the removal of staff from classes to mentor individual pupils:

> *On the one hand you're asking the staff to work hard, teach well, to work to overall school targets; on the other hand you have to actually take them out of lessons to do it. There's a big contradiction between that.* (project coordinator)

4.6 Experience of mentored pupils and parents

This section highlights the experiences of mentoring programmes for both pupils and their parents. It begins by outlining the way in which pupils from the case-study schools were informed and involved in the initial stages of the programme. It then describes pupils' perceptions of their mentoring programme. A description of the perceived benefits and limitations of mentoring for pupils follow this. The final section describes the involvement and views of parents in relation to their child's mentoring programme.

Involving pupils

Once staff had identified the pupils that they wanted to target, they either assembled them for a meeting or approached them on an individual basis to inform them about the programme and ask them if they wanted to participate.

Staff at roughly half of the schools stated that it was important to present the programme to the targeted pupils in a positive light to encourage pupils to participate and appreciate the possible benefits that mentoring could have for them. At two schools, staff considered the positive presentation of the strategy to be so important to the success of the strategy that they were willing to be slightly underhand; they took the conscious decision not to tell pupils that they were specifically targeting those who were underachieving. Interestingly, Golden and Sims (1997) also noted that the staff in their study considered it important for schemes to be presented positively to pupils to encourage participation and reduce the risk of pupils being negatively labelled.

At a number of the schools, interviews with both staff and pupils indicated that they believed that in order for mentoring to work effectively pupils had to be both committed and motivated to the programme. In an attempt to ensure this, in six of the schools, pupil participation in mentoring programmes was done on a voluntary rather than compulsory basis:

> *It should be voluntary because people are wasting teachers' time if they don't want to do it.* (Year 11 boy)

In most of these schools, staff stated that the majority of pupils who were asked to participate in the programme accepted the opportunity. On occasion, staff at two schools stated that if a targeted pupil declined the opportunity to take part they would apply a little bit of pressure initially so that the pupil attended at least a few sessions before making a final decision. If someone finally decided against participating in a programme, their place was usually offered to some one else:

> *We were picked out to be mentored but we could have turned it down and the mentoring would have been offered to someone else.* (Year 11 girl)

At the two other schools, one of which focused on all Year 10 pupils, all targeted pupils were expected to partake in the programme.

Pupils' reactions to mentoring

In about half of the case study schools, interviews with staff and pupils revealed that pupils generally held positive perceptions of their mentoring programmes. However, in the remaining schools, staff and pupils expressed a wide range of different reactions. For example, in some schools, there was a relatively low take-up of places and a number of pupils dropped out.

At roughly half of the schools, senior members of staff stated that they did not think that targeted pupils experienced any negative peer pressure because they were being mentored:

> [They are] *used to people coming into lessons to support special needs and they're used to going out as well; they go out for a whole range of things and a whole range of them go out, so I don't think there's any big deal attached to it.* (project coordinator)

However, at a few of these schools, some pupils said that some of their peers who were not participating in schemes perceived the participation of others in a derogatory way.

In over half of the schools, staff noted that some pupils, especially girls, who were not specifically targeted to take part in mentoring programmes asked if they could participate. At a few schools, this was possible but staff at other schools stated that they had to pacify these pupils by explaining that they were on target to fulfil their potential and therefore did not need to be mentored:

> *Some girls felt that their noses had been pushed out of joint because they weren't having the same access.* (project coordinator)

The perceived benefits of mentoring for pupils

Interviews with staff and pupils at the case study schools revealed that mentoring had both academic and social benefits for pupils. At the academic level, staff at a few schools noted that mentoring helped to improve pupils' learning skills by providing them with extra support and extra tuition on how to manage their time effectively, organise their workload and complete their coursework to the best of their ability. For boys, the main academic benefits centred around issues of more efficient organisation, whilst for girls, they tended to centre around managing the pressures of workload, learning to write succinctly and a wide range of more individual issues.

For staff at the majority of schools, the other main benefit of mentoring for pupils was considered to operate at the social level. In all schools, staff felt that mentoring enabled pupils to feel cared for, by explicitly allocating them someone with whom they could discuss problems and issues, a form of support which was often overlooked or considered impractical within many schools:

> *I think a lot of boys have definitely benefited from it noticeably. Some of the boys in my class certainly have; they really respond to that extra attention that they wouldn't otherwise get.*
>
> (staff mentor)

In addition, both staff and pupils felt that the one-to-one relationship provided through mentoring helped to increase pupils' levels of confidence, self-esteem, motivation and attitudes to school and learning, which encouraged pupils to take responsibility for their learning:

> *They would never have thought of their performance and their own achievements if they didn't have a member of staff to actually sit down and discuss those issues with ... [it] gives them much*

added confidence in their own ability and their own achievement because they're much more focused on their weaknesses.

(staff mentor)

If you're on the verge of getting five Cs, then this can be that extra push to getting them. (Year 11 girl)

More specifically, staff at a number of schools believed that mentoring helped to challenge some boys' stereotypical anti-school attitudes, which encouraged them to value the importance of learning:

Without a shadow of a doubt I think a lot of boys find themselves marginalised by school ... I think that it's important to make them feel [that] *to achieve academically is something they should be proud of rather than something they should avoid because it doesn't accord with their street credibility.* (staff mentor)

At most of these schools, staff felt that due to the academic and social impact that mentoring had on pupils, it inevitably had a positive influence on their achievement and thus the overall performance of the school:

I think the benefits have got to be the improvements they see in their grades. Nathan is absolutely over the moon. Not even his parents thought that he could possibly get five A – Cs. It's also a benefit for us if it helps to improve our pass rates. (staff mentor)

We're happy because at the end of the day we get time to target children who are underachieving which improves the school's exam results. If it goes well then, you know, everyone seems to benefit (project coordinator)

The perceived limitations of mentoring for pupils

Staff and pupils at the case study schools identified a number of limitations regarding their mentoring schemes. These limitations centred on the way in which schemes were implemented and structured and on the relationship between mentors and pupils.

For example, in the seven schools which targeted specific groups of pupils within certain year groups, a primary limitation was the fact that the programme was not available to *all* pupils, especially girls:

[The focus on underachieving pupils/boys] *produced an uncomfortable feeling amongst some because the school had always prided itself on treating everyone equally. They didn't like this focus on the C – D borderline. However, because our results aren't, or weren't, going up like other schools in the area, there was a realisation that we would have to start doing this type of thing.* (project coordinator)

In addition, staff at two of these schools also noted that the identification of pupils for participation in their mentoring programme was not always scientific.

Confirming the findings of previous research (such as Golden and Sims, 1997), staff and pupils in over half of the case study schools also felt that mentoring sessions were neither frequent enough nor long enough and, in some cases, were not very well structured. For staff, this meant that it was difficult to get some pupils, especially those of lower ability, to open up and participate fully in the session, which led to some pupils failing to experience the full benefits of mentoring.

For some pupils, this meant that they often felt that they did not get a chance to contribute to the target-setting process but found themselves simply agreeing with mentors. Some pupils also felt that there was not sufficient time for them to discuss strategies for achieving their targets with their mentors.

At a number of schools, it was noted that problems arose when mentors and pupils were not paired together appropriately. It was felt that both staff and pupils should be given some choice in who their partners were in order to facilitate good mentoring. At a number of schools, it was also felt that if mentors were not committed, this could have an adverse effect on pupils who would sometimes perceive a mentor's lack of commitment as a personal affront. This confirms the findings of previous research (Golden and Sims, 1997), which concluded that the sudden departure of out-of-school mentors can have a negative effect on some pupils who may feel that mentors drop out because of something that they have done.

The involvement and views of parents

At seven of the case study schools, once pupils had agreed to take part in the mentoring programme, a letter was sent to their parents. The letters informed parents about the programme and about their child's participation in it. Letters from four of the schools invited parents to attend a meeting where they could find out more about the school's mentoring scheme (see Appendix 4.6). At a few schools, parents were asked to sign a contract which represented a recognition that their child was taking part in the programme and indicated that the parents were willing to support their child and the school in achieving the aims of the programme.

Three of these schools also sent letters out from time to time informing parents of their child's progress in the programme and, at one school, if their child no longer needed to participate in the scheme. A number of schools also used parents' evenings as an opportunity to discuss the scheme and pupils' progress.

In general, at the majority of schools, staff and pupils stated that parents were supportive and enthusiastic about the schemes and perceived mentoring to be of benefit to their child. This was primarily because their child was receiving individual attention and support:

I was met by a sort of helpful, overwhelming, tidal wave of relief on the part of the parents, many of whom seemed to almost be at their wits end with their sons' indifference.   (project coordinator)

My parents were really pleased because she always thought that I got so worked up about my work and this made it easier.

(Year 11 girl)

4.7   Evaluating the effectiveness of mentoring programmes

This section highlights the case study schools' evaluation of their mentoring programmes. It begins by describing the different systems that schools have in place for evaluating their programmes and then presents the evidence from schools regarding the success of their programmes. Key factors for the success of projects are then highlighted and this is followed by the suggestions of staff on possible changes to their programmes in the future.

Evidence regarding the success of mentoring programmes

As in the schools experimenting with single-sex classes, the schools that had implemented mentoring also used a combination of quantitative and qualitative approaches to monitor the effectiveness of their programmes. Quantitative data included information from GCSE examination results, key stage tests, reading tests and records of mentoring sessions which included data on attendance, punctuality, behavioural incidents and pupil achievement of targets.

Five of the six case study schools targeting pupils at KS4 had GCSE examination results which showed that the targeted pupils had, overall, achieved better grades than had been predicted – primarily in terms of the number of five or more A – Cs. The remaining school did not yet have any evidence in terms of GCSE results as the mentoring programme had only recently been implemented.

For example, at Bacon Comprehensive, during 1997 – 98, seven out of 18 mentored pupils who were predicted to achieve five or more Ds or above actually achieved five grade Cs. Similarly, at Abbott High, 11 pupils were identified as being on the borderline of four to five or more C grades following their mock examinations and were offered the opportunity to take part in the mentoring programme. Of the nine pupils who participated in the programme, six gained five or more C grades. In contrast the two male pupils who declined the opportunity to be mentored achieved two or less grade Cs at GCSE.

At Epstein Secondary, the impact of mentoring was also being monitored through additional forms of quantitative evidence such as: attendance rates, which were calculated on a monthly basis; the number of fixed exclusions, for both boys and girls; and monthly collations of incident report sheets, which highlighted the gender of the pupil, the subject teacher who referred the pupil and the reason for the referral. An evaluation of these monitoring systems had yet to be completed.

At the two schools targeting pupils in Year 8, although initial results looked positive – in terms of reading test scores and end-of-year reports – staff felt it was too early to assess the impact of their schemes.

Over half of the case study schools also used qualitative approaches to evaluate the impact of mentoring on their pupils. These approaches included the use of pupil and staff evaluations – via focus groups, questionnaires and interviews – end-of-year reports and feedback from parents (see Appendices 4.7 and 4.8). In general, staff, parents and pupils perceived mentoring to be of benefit, although suggestions for improvement were often made, such as making the programme more structured and starting the programme earlier. Illustration 4.4 below describes how one school used the qualitative approach of interviewing pupils to evaluate the impact of mentoring.

Illustration 4.4:   A qualitative approach to evaluating the impact of mentoring

At Flaxman Comprehensive, following the first year of the mentoring programme, the school's pastoral adviser interviewed the pupils who had participated on the programme in order to assess their reactions. Roughly half of the pupils were interviewed individually and half were interviewed in small groups of four to six pupils. In summary, the programme was generally understood and welcomed by the pupils. Pupils' views about the usefulness of the programme ranged from positive to negative. Some of the pupils recognised that they would benefit more from the scheme if they put more effort into it themselves. The majority of the pupils felt that the programme could be improved if sessions were more frequent or if pupils were more regularly reminded, on an informal basis, of the need to keep to their targets, and if mentors were more specific about ways in which pupils could achieve their targets.

Providing independent evidence to substantiate the tentative, initial findings regarding the positive impact of mentoring, recent OFSTED reports on two of these schools noted:

The school is making strenuous efforts to raise performance ... it is using strategies such as mentoring students in Y11 to help them organise their learning and study skills in order to improve their chances in examinations (p. 6) ... this is appreciated by pupils and has a positive effect on standards of achievement.

(OFSTED, 1997)

The school has succeeded in motivating boys and raising their levels of achievement. ... The gap between the relative achievements of boys and girls narrowed in 1998 from 10% to 4%, when comparing the proportion gaining 5 or more GCSE grades A* – C. Support groups for more able students, mentoring arrangements and effective monitoring help to ensure that all students, irrespective of gender, ethnicity or ability, are encouraged to achieve their full potential. (OFSTED, 1999)

At three of the case study schools, staff noted that the impact of mentoring had helped them to reduce their gender gap in achievement. However, at one school, where mentoring was available to both boys and girls who were on the five A – C borderline, staff felt that mentoring had worked along with other raising achievement strategies to improve the performance of girls as well, thus maintaining or increasing the gender gap in performance:

We had a 20 per cent gender gap three years ago, 15 per cent two years ago, and our target this last year was ten per cent – we didn't get that; in fact, we got a 23 per cent gender gap! So all the raising standards work we did improved results, but it improved the results of girls, as opposed to boys, by a large proportion.
(project coordinator)

At the remaining four schools, mentoring programmes had not been in place long enough for staff to assess their impact on gender differences in achievement and at one of these schools, staff did not feel that their system of monitoring provided them with the necessary evidence to comment.

The findings of previous research have recognised that one of the major limitations of mentoring schemes is that they are difficult to evaluate. For example, the study by Golden and Sims (1997) showed that although the vast majority of the schemes under investigation were evaluated through questionnaires, NCA test results, anecdotal evidence and record keeping, it was not possible for the researchers to derive any firm evidence regarding the effectiveness of the schemes. However, they did note that the key participants generally expressed satisfaction. Golden and Sims (1997) therefore concluded that there was

Difficulty with attributing with certainty any change in student behaviour or performance directly to the experience of mentoring'
(p.18).

At a few of the case study schools, staff noted that although pupils appeared to do better than expected, it was difficult to attribute this specifically to the impact of mentoring, firstly, because of the difficulties associated with mentoring and evaluating a strategy that was either recently established or recently modified; and secondly, because participation on a mentoring programme represents just one of a wealth of factors which combine in complex ways to impinge on pupil achievement:

I think it's a question of whether a boy, say, would have achieved the same results without the mentoring and that's difficult to prove.

(staff mentor)

It has been suggested that the difficulties associated with evaluating mentoring programmes arise from the fact that mentoring has yet to be clearly conceptualised, which leads to confusion about what mentoring actually represents (Merriam, 1983) and because evaluation practices are not standardised across all schools (Beattie and Holden, 1994). It has therefore been suggested that the only way to evaluate mentoring schemes is in relation to their objectives (Monaghan, 1992), the effects of which are not always quantifiable as they address different issues for different people (Golden and Sims, 1997; Beattie and Holden, 1994). As a result, Merriam (1983) suggests that formal mentoring programmes need to be evaluated more extensively before conclusions can be reached as to their value.

Future changes

Staff at the case study schools identified a number of modifications that they were considering making in the future. The most popular idea was to extend the scheme to other pupils – either to those in other years within the school or to other pupils not currently targeted. In addition, staff from different schools stated that they would like to improve procedures for staff training and guidance, tighten up the efficiency of the mentoring scheme, try and involve parents more fully and improve monitoring and evaluation procedures. Staff at two schools stated that the continuation of the schemes at their schools was dependent on finding funding for the future.

4.8 Summary

This chapter has highlighted the way in which eight secondary schools used the strategy of mentoring to address gender differences in achievement. The main findings from this chapter regarding the use and efficacy of this strategy are summarised below. A summary describing the way one case study school used mentoring is provided in Appendix 4.9.

Rationale

♦ Schools often took the decision to address the issue of gender differences in achievement because they were aware of gaps in performance in their own schools and recognised that girls' outperformance of boys was of national interest and concern. The strategy of mentoring was chosen for three main reasons: firstly, because mentoring enabled schools to target specific pupils, such as those who were underachieving (most of whom were boys); secondly, because mentoring provided an opportunity to help pupils tackle the specific weaknesses that they had; and thirdly, because mentoring was seen as one way of improving pupils' orientation towards school and learning through the use of a one-to-one relationship and/or positive role models.

The focus of mentoring programmes

♦ Schools tended to target pupils in relation to where gender differences were prevalent within the schools. Differences were often found at GCSE level in terms of the number of boys, compared to girls, achieving five or more A – C grades. Schools therefore tended to focus on pupils in KS4 who were on the five or more A – C borderline.

♦ Teachers were also conscious that they did not want to raise the achievement of boys at the expense of girls and made every effort to open programmes up, at the very least, to all pupils who met the selection criteria.

♦ Mentoring programmes generally had similar characteristics. They often ran for a year and generally took place once or twice a week for 20 minutes out of lesson time. Pupils were usually mentored on a one-to-one basis by a staff mentor. Sessions often included a review of progress made by pupils in relation to targets set at the last session, discussion of pupils' current strengths and weaknesses both academically and socially, and the setting of new targets in relation to what had been discussed.

Implementing programmes

♦ Training had to be provided for mentors in order to explain the programme, outline the role of mentors and to highlight the different strategies that mentors could use when mentoring. Funding had to be found to cover administration costs and, on occasion, staff time. Following the pilots of programmes, modifications were often made which included providing mentors with guidelines and improving the efficacy of the paperwork associated with the programme.

Key participants

♦ Mentors often participated on a voluntary basis, and as a result it was often difficult to find an appropriate time to provide mentors with training. This meant that pupils often received mentoring of variable quality. Over time, mentors became increasingly convinced of the benefits of mentoring.

♦ It was considered important that the programme was presented to pupils in a positive light in order to counter any negative reactions. Although pupils were targeted, their participation was often on a voluntary basis as it was necessary for pupils to be committed and motivated in order for them to benefit fully from the programme.

♦ Mentoring was perceived as beneficial for pupils as it helped them to address the weaknesses in their learning styles. For boys, this often meant that they became more organised and learnt how to manage their time effectively, whilst for girls, this usually meant that they developed strategies for dealing with the pressures of work. In addition, the one-to-one relationship with a mentor helped to build pupils' levels of confidence, self-esteem and motivation, which challenged the anti-learning subculture that some teachers felt was prevalent among some groups of boys.

♦ The main limitations of mentoring centred around organisational constraints such as not being able to offer the programme to all pupils and sessions not being frequent nor long enough. Some pupils also admitted to experiencing negative peer pressure.

♦ Parents were usually kept informed of their child's participation and progress in the programme. In general, it was perceived that parents considered mentoring to be of benefit to their children.

Evaluation of programmes

♦ Evaluations of the programmes revealed that mentoring appeared to be working in terms of enabling pupils to fulfil their potential, which helped to address gender gaps in performance. However, in roughly half of the case study schools, staff did not feel confident about assessing the impact of their mentoring programmes because they had not been in place for a long enough period, had recently been modified, or because of difficulties associated with evaluating them.

In summary, the following list highlights the main factors which staff and pupils considered essential for the effective implementation of mentoring programmes.

KEY FACTORS THAT MAKE MENTORING PROGRAMMES WORK

- presenting the strategy positively to the pupils so that they do not feel stigmatised and appreciate its potential benefits;

- pupils have to want to take part in the programme so that they are both committed and motivated;

- mentors and pupils must have a strong relationship built on trust and a good rapport;

- mentors need to be committed, enthusiastic and supportive towards the concept of mentoring for it to work to full effect;

- mentors are given appropriate training and support so that they can appreciate the aims and objectives of their school's mentoring programme and therefore run the programme effectively;

- programmes are carefully organised, coordinated and resourced, and efforts are made to enable them to become embedded within the culture of the school, in order for mentoring to have maximum impact across all curriculum areas;

- programmes are carefully monitored and evaluated so they can be modified annually in relation to the differing needs of the pupils being targeted.

5. ADDITIONAL LITERACY SUPPORT

5.1 Setting the context

In a recent OFSTED review of gender differences in achievement (Arnot *et al.*, 1998), it was noted that one of the three main areas where gaps are prominent is in early literacy skills and later on in English, where girls generally outperform boys. The review reveals that girls establish a clear advantage over boys in reading at KS1 and maintain this lead at key stages 2 and 3. Confirming these claims, a recent report by the Qualifications and Curriculum Authority (QCA) (1998) stated that in the results of the National Curriculum assessment tests in 1997, 21 per cent of girls, compared with 14 per cent of boys, achieved level 3 or above in KS1 English. At KS2, 69 per cent of girls, compared with 57 per cent of boys, achieved level 4 or above in English.

In an attempt to address concerns about pupil achievement in literacy, David Blunkett, the then shadow Secretary of State for Education and Employment, established a National Literacy Task Force in 1996. The Task Force devised a National Literacy Strategy, the main aim of which was to substantially raise the standard of literacy in primary schools over five to ten years. The main target of the strategy is to ensure that by the year 2002, 80 per cent of all 11-year-olds reaches the standard expected for their age (level 4) in KS2 National Curriculum assessment tests (GB. DFEE, 1997).

The findings from research in this area suggest that there are three main explanations for the gender differential in pupils' literacy achievement. Firstly, it has been argued that from pre-school on, boys develop a learning style in which they are more predisposed towards active learning methods. Consequently some boys tend to be less reflective and find it difficult to concentrate on a task at length, traits which tend to inhibit the development of literacy skills from the early years (QCA, 1998).

Secondly, research has shown that boys and girls have distinct reading preferences which lead them to develop writing styles which are differentially valued within the current education system. For example, it has been argued (Bleach, 1998b) that boys prefer reading non-fiction books that often relate to their hobby interests whilst girls' tastes in reading include a substantial amount of fiction. However, because the National Curriculum is based more on fiction, than non-fiction there is less reading material that appeals to boys (MacDonald *et al.*, 1999). As a result, some boys become disillusioned with reading as the types of books that they are interested in, and the writing styles that they develop as a result of them, are not valued within the National Curriculum.

Thirdly, it has been argued (QCA, 1998; Wiltshire Education Support & Training, 1996) that English is perceived by pupils to be a 'feminine' subject. This is partly because it relates to traits traditionally associated with women, such as personal response, discussion and reflectiveness, and partly because the majority of adults who read with young children, such as primary school teachers, primary school assistants and mothers, all tend to be female, which means that young boys see few positive male role models in relation to literacy. It is therefore suggested that boys are turned off from English at an early age because they perceive it as a 'girls' subject'. Peer group pressure works to reinforce these perceptions, making it increasingly difficult for boys to be seen to succeed in the subject (QCA, 1998).

A recent report by QCA (1998) suggested that the strategy of additional literacy support could be used as one way to address these issues and thus counter the discrepancy in the literacy performance of boys and girls: firstly, because additional reading sessions can provide boys with the opportunity to read materials which are often ignored within the classroom but which boys find interesting (such as non-fiction and comics); and secondly, because one-to-one literacy support enables pupils to discuss what they have read and to obtain constructive feedback, continuous recognition and praise within an unpressurised environment, leading to an increase in confidence, motivation and ability.

This chapter attempts to build on the work of such research by presenting the way in which three primary schools used additional literacy support to address pupils', especially boys', underachievement in literacy. Like the previous chapters, this chapter will explain why staff decided to adopt the strategy of additional literacy support, how it was used within their school and how it was implemented. It will then highlight the involvement and experiences of staff, additional literacy supporters and pupils. Finally, there is an examination of how effective additional literacy support has been within the schools along with a summary of the key factors that have made it successful.

5.2 Rationale for utilising additional literacy support

Staff at the three primary schools decided to tackle the issue of pupil underachievement in literacy for a number of reasons: firstly, because they were aware of the long-running national debate surrounding the issue; and secondly, because they recognised that certain groups of children within their schools, who were usually boys, were consistently underachieving in literacy. This recognition was often based on evidence from NCA results. Staff therefore felt that standards could be raised, and gender differences in achievement addressed, if pupil underachievement in literacy was tackled.

In response to these concerns, staff across all three schools considered ways of raising pupils', and especially boys', levels of literacy and decided that it could most effectively be addressed by enhancing pupils' attitudes towards, and confidence in, literacy rather than by focusing directly on improving their skills:

> *It is definitely not raising the skill of reading; it is raising their appreciation of reading.* (headteacher)

Staff within the schools felt that they could fulfil these objectives by adopting, or building, on their use of additional support from adult volunteers. Taking this approach would enable pupils to receive one-to-one help for concentrated periods of time, which they would not otherwise be able to get. In addition, some staff stated that this enabled the emphasis to be taken off the learning process and put on to the enjoyment of literacy, which provided pupils with a relaxed environment that was conducive to building their self-esteem, confidence and enthusiasm about literacy:

> *It also raises children's self-esteem as well as their actual reading levels because they get this attention from an adult that they would never normally get in school.* (headteacher)

Within the research on boys' underachievement in literacy, it has been suggested (Noble, 1998) that the use of male role models may be of benefit to some boys in terms of challenging their traditional stereotypical perceptions of literacy as 'feminine'. Reflecting this belief, the headteacher at one of the case study schools noted:

> *The thing that attracted us to this formalised approach was that they* [the adult supporters] *were men, because we have lots of parents that work here, lots of other volunteers that work in the school, but they are all women and we wanted a model for the boys. We've actually got a clump of boys who are having difficulties with reading so we needed them to see men reading.* (headteacher)

5.3 How schools use additional literacy support.

The use of additional adult support to improve pupils' levels of literacy had only been implemented relatively recently (in 1997 or 1998) within the three schools. Literacy supporters usually came into school for blocks of five to six weeks (half a term) for an hour, usually at a time that was convenient for them. In general, they would work with three children on an individual basis, one to three times a week, for 15 – 30 minutes each. Pupils usually participated in schemes for one block of sessions (half a term). At the end of each block, class teachers would use a combination of professional judgement and the results of reading tests to decide whether pupils should be kept on the scheme or taken off to provide space for another child. Within schools, staff were able to bring children back on to the scheme at a later date, depending on their needs.

The role of additional literacy supporters across all schools was to listen to, and help, pupils read. They usually also had the wider role of firstly, supporting pupils' literacy development, through strategies such as asking questions about books; and secondly, of increasing pupils' interest and enthusiasm for reading through the materials used and games such as word searches and crosswords:

The main thing was to add a bit of fun to reading, to make it a pleasure and not a chore, to give the children a little bit of confidence reading out loud. (parent literacy supporter)

You are supposed to work with each child and get them to do a bit of reading, but there are also games to play like word searches. It's supposed to be to try and make reading more fun for the children and to try to get them to read.

(supporter from the VRH Scheme)

One school also used its own staff, the SENCO and a learning support assistant to provide pupils with literacy support. These supporters developed specific work schemes for use with small groups of two to five pupils and provided them with more formal forms of support. As in the case of most additional literacy support, this support was also given in 20-minute sessions three times a week. One pupil reflected:

We look at alphabets and words, we have to see someone out of class time three times a week to learn to spell properly, put letters together to make words and then read. (Year 3 pupil)

In general, all literacy support sessions took place during lesson time either within the child's classroom (in a quiet corner) or in a quiet available space, such as the library. The illustration below provides one example of a literacy session within one of the case study schools.

Illustration 5.1: A literacy support session

A one-to-one literacy session between an adult, from the Volunteer Reading Help Scheme, and a Year 6 pupil was observed at Asquith school. The session lasted for 25 minutes and took place in a quiet corner of the library.

The volunteer collected the pupil from her class and they walked across to the well-decorated library and sat at a table in the corner. The volunteer opened up the red box of materials that had been provided by the Reading Help Scheme and took out a selection of books. Throughout this time, the volunteer and the pupil chatted about what the pupil had been doing recently both in and outside of school. The conversation was conducted on a friendly, informal basis and was punctuated with laughter.

The volunteer asked the pupil to choose a book from the box. Once the pupil had made her selection, she opened the book and began to read to the volunteer. Whenever the pupil got to a word that she did not know, the volunteer used a number of strategies to help her work it out, such as encouraging her to sound out each part of the word, or suggesting that she look for clues in the accompanying picture. Whilst the pupil read, the volunteer provided her with encouragement, praise and stimulation by asking her questions about what she was reading.

The pupil completed the short story after 15 minutes. The volunteer then took out a book of crosswords and they chose a puzzle to complete. The pupil would read the clue, think of the answer and write it into the appropriate space. The volunteer helped her with difficult words, provided her with, additional clues, when necessary, and on occasion would help the pupil to spell words that she did not know. After they had finished the puzzle, the bell went, they said their goodbyes and the pupil went back to her class.

The volunteer and the pupil had clearly developed a trusting and supportive relationship over the 14 months that they had worked together. The pupil spoke confidently to the volunteer on a formal and informal basis. She was not afraid to ask the volunteer questions nor embarrassed to accept his help.

The pupils targeted

The three schools targeted pupils from a range of year groups for participation in their schemes, and all focused on specific subgroups of pupils within these year groups. The number of pupils targeted by schools varied according to the number of additional literacy supporters that schools were able to use at any given time. Table 5.1 below summarises the different pupils targeted by the case study schools.

Table 5.1: The different pupils targeted for additional literacy support

School	Year groups	Pupils targeted	Process of identification	No. of pupils
Asquith Primary	Years 2–6	Those who were underachieving or lacked confidence in reading	Reading tests	35
Baldwin School	Year 3	Low achievers in reading	Variety of test results	10
	Years 4 – 5	Various	N/A	Various
Callaghan Primary	Years 2 – 6	Those who would benefit from additional literacy support	Teacher judgement	10

At Asquith Primary, staff targeted pupils who were either underachieving or lacked confidence in reading. Initially, staff focused on pupils who were in the higher years of key stage 2 (Years 5 and 6) but as the school recruited increasing numbers of additional literacy supporters, they expanded their target population to include similar types of pupils from Years 2, 4, 5 and 6. To identify these pupils, staff used the results of reading tests which pupils completed twice a year. At the time of this study (1998 – 1999), the school was using seven volunteers from the Business Partnership Scheme and two volunteers from the Volunteer Reading Help Scheme to provide 35 pupils with additional literacy support.

At Baldwin School, staff targeted the ten pupils who were the lowest achievers in reading in Year 3. Staff at this school used a combination of test results (NCAs, PIPS, reading tests) to identify these pupils, who were then put into small groups of two to five to receive additional support, according to their needs, from the school's SENCO and learning support assistant. In addition, a number of pupils from Years 4 and 5 were provided with additional literacy support from local volunteers in an attempt to improve their reading.

At Callaghan Primary, pupils were targeted from across key stages 1 and 2 (Years 2 to 6). The class teachers of these year groups were asked each half a term to use their professional judgement to identify two pupils who they thought would benefit, either academically or socially, from additional support for literacy. The majority of these pupils tended to be boys. A classteacher noted:

> We tried to identify which children would benefit most: those children who found reading a chore, were reluctant to read a book or had to be pushed into talking about books ... we tried to home in on boys in particular to get them involved in reading books because you know, throughout key stage 2, if you look at the children, the boys show a reluctance.   (class teacher)

As a result, ten pupils from across the year groups were provided with the opportunity to receive additional literacy support form ten parent helpers for a half-term block of sessions.

Although staff at the three case study schools used a systematic approach in order to identify underachieving pupils, two of the schools relied predominantly on reading test results. However, within the QCA (1998) report, it was noted that the identification of pupils for extra literacy support needs to be carefully considered as a sole reliance on standardised test scores may mean that the abilities which boys show in reading non-fiction texts are neglected. It is interesting to note that staff within the primary schools, unlike many staff within the secondary schools referred to in earlier chapters, did not specifically target 'borderline' pupils (i.e. Year 2 pupils on the border of levels one and two in KS1 NCA tests and Year 6 pupils on the border of levels three and four in KS2 NCA tests).

5.4 The process of implementation

This section outlines the way in which staff implemented the use of additional literacy support within their schools, in terms of the practical preparations made, the training provided for supporters and obtaining funds to support the strategy.

Practical preparations

None of the three schools had to make any changes to their timetables in order to use additional literacy support as all sessions took place during lesson time. One school had initially attempted to schedule all sessions during assembly time, but this proved inappropriate as pupils ended up missing out on too many things. So like the other schools, sessions were rescheduled to take place during lessons at a time that was convenient to the additional literacy supporters.

Sessions were often arranged to take place either in part of a classroom or in a quiet available place such as the library. However, a number of additional literacy supporters noted that due to the limitations of space within primary schools, it was often difficult to find an appropriate place in which to have sessions.

Training additional literacy supporters

Additional literacy supporters who were provided to Asquith Primary through national schemes, such as Business Partnership Schemes or the Volunteer Reading Help (VRH) Scheme, were provided with formal training through the schemes. This often included information about the scheme and basic advice, from experts in the field, about providing literacy support for children. The VRH scheme also provided volunteers with regular training to update their skills throughout the year, which volunteers found useful.

The schools which relied on parent and local community volunteers did not provide these additional literacy supporters with any formal training. However, at Callaghan Primary, parent volunteers were given introductory sessions where they were provided with information regarding their perceived role in the scheme and advice from an LEA adviser about possible strategies to use to get the best out of the children. The headteacher noted that the involvement of the LEA adviser helped to provide the scheme with status, which made parent volunteers appreciate its importance.

Staff and additional literacy supporters felt that an important component of training was to ensure that key participants were made explicitly aware of the role of additional literacy supporters and therefore recognised that

> *it is the teacher's job to teach; the parents are just assisting.*
> (headteacher):

> *It's quite basic, I'm not trained to teach, I'm just here to help them with their reading and to complement what's going on in class.* (volunteer)

Funding

In order to implement strategies, two schools had to purchase new books which specifically targeted reluctant and boy readers. One of these schools also had to find funds to redecorate the library so that it was a more welcoming place, as some sessions were scheduled to take place there. Staff at one school were able to meet the costs of additional resources by putting in a bid to their LEA Boys' Achievement Project, for which they received £1,000. The other school was able to pay for its resources through £1,000 which was raised by the parents of its pupils and funds from the school's literacy budget.

The third school did not have to obtain any funding for additional resources in order to facilitate the use of additional literacy supporters. This was partly because the school used adult supporters from the VRH scheme, which provided their volunteers with a box of resources such as books, games and puzzles which they could use with the children.

5.5 The involvement and experiences of key participants

This section outlines the way in which staff, additional literacy supporters, pupils and parents were involved in the strategy. It also highlights their general perceptions of the strengths and weaknesses of using additional literacy support.

The involvement and views of staff

In all three schools, the headteacher had overall responsibility for arranging the recruitment and use of additional literacy supporters. In two of the schools, SENCOs, and in one school, class teachers had responsibility for identifying which children would have the opportunity to receive additional literacy support. The two SENCOs also had responsibility for monitoring progress through the use of regular reading tests. The role of the class teacher was generally to facilitate the withdrawal of children from their class for literacy support sessions. This could be difficult as children were withdrawn at various times – at the convenience of the additional literacy supporter.

In terms of lesson time, I am careful to organise things so that when the children were out of class I was doing similar work with the children left in the class so that the withdrawn children didn't feel like they were missing anything. (class teacher)

The role of non-teachers in the classroom can be a contentious issue, as Caudrey (1985) points out:

Some teachers believe the presence of parents in the classroom can be beneficial and may even enhance the status of the teacher. But, others resent amateurs encroaching on their professional territory, as well as claiming the exercise gives local authorities an excuse to keep down staffing levels (p.17).

In the case study schools, although some staff were initially reluctant about the use of additional literacy supporters, over time they became increasingly convinced of its benefits for both pupils and for themselves. A number noted that one of the main benefits of using additional literacy supporters was that it took the pressure off class teachers to ensure that these pupils were receiving the level of support and attention that they needed:

As a class teacher, the benefits are that the children are getting more time reading to someone and discussing books, having that three times a week – you'd never be able to give that time and attention as a class teacher. (class teacher)

Overall, staff across all three schools felt that the use of additional literacy supporters had little negative impact on their workloads.

Additional literacy supporters: their recruitment, involvement and experience

Previous research into the use of parental support has claimed that there is a strong correlation between parents' socio-economic status and the extent to which they are willing to be involved in their child's education (Topping, 1986). Topping has suggested that the use of parental support can serve to *'add another string to the bow of middle-class educational advantage'* as schools in less affluent areas are less likely to have parents who are willing to volunteer time and therefore miss out on the benefits that additional adult (parental) support can bring.

The staff in the three case study schools, which were all situated within predominantly working-class areas, did not rely solely on parent volunteers as they were able to recruit additional literacy supporters from a wide range of sources, such as:

♦ national organisations (i.e. Volunteer Reading Help Scheme);

♦ local authority business partnership schemes;

♦ additional staff (e.g. SENCOs and learning support assistants);

♦ the local community (e.g. volunteers from a local church group); and

♦ parent volunteers.

Only Callaghan Primary relied completely on the parents and other family members of its pupils to volunteer to take on the role of literacy supporter. In order to recruit people, they sent a letter out to all parents requesting help and emphasising the need for commitment to the strategy. Staff noted that, initially, it was difficult to convey to parents the main aims of the scheme and what would be required of parent volunteers, making it difficult to generate enthusiasm and interest in the scheme. However, in the first year, they were able to recruit ten parents who were willing to commit themselves to a half-term block of sessions.

Across the three schools, the additional literacy supporters committed themselves to participating in schemes for various lengths of time depending on how the scheme was organised within the school. For example, some supporters (i.e. VRH scheme) worked for a full year within a school often with the same children whilst other literacy supporters (e.g. volunteers from business partnership schemes and parents) committed themselves to working for variable numbers of five to six session blocks, with many participating for over six months. The adult literacy volunteers usually went into schools at a regular time that was convenient to themselves.

Topping's study (1986) of parental support found that volunteers felt that they had benefited from taking part in schemes as they considered it important to have supported a child's education, had acquired new skills, had developed greater community awareness and found participation personally satisfying.

Within the case study schools, similar views were found. Additional literacy supporters, from local and national organisations, stated that they enjoyed their role because it provided them with an opportunity to find out how schools are run and what pupils are taught and it allowed them to help schools make links with the wider community. In addition, parent literacy supporters also noted that they saw volunteering as an opportunity to help the school by giving something back.

Pupils' experiences of additional literacy support

The extent to which staff explicitly informed pupils about their possible participation in different schemes depended on the degree to which schemes were open to all pupils. Where schemes were organised in a way which meant that most pupils would at some point participate in the scheme, there was a general openness and all pupils were told about the scheme and that they would all probably participate in it at some point (Callaghan Primary). However, where schemes were targeted at very specific groups of pupils, such as the ten lowest achievers (Baldwin School), staff adopted a more low-key approach to informing pupils.

Previous research (Topping, 1986; Tower Hamlets EBP, 1998) has found that the use of additional literacy supporters provides pupils with increased opportunities to expand their use of language, which helps to increase their levels of confidence enabling pupils to participate more actively in lessons.

Reflecting these findings, across all three schools staff felt that the main benefit of additional literacy support for pupils was that it provided pupils with one-to-one support or more direct attention which made them feel that someone was specifically interested in them. Like the one-to-one mentoring discussed in Chapter 4, staff felt that this form of support helped to increase these children's levels of motivation, confidence and self-esteem; this impacted positively on their attitudes towards, and skills in, literacy. The increased confidence of children in their literacy abilities was also felt to have led to their increased participation in class activities.

Some staff also noted that pupils' improved skills in literacy also had a positive impact on their levels of achievement in other subject areas, as well as on their behaviour:

The knock-on effect is tremendous for the rest of the subjects because no matter what subject, you've got to have some element of reading. (class teacher)

The main benefit, apart from the reading ages going up, has been in terms of behaviour in the classroom. They are not as disruptive as they were and they do sit and listen more. (class teacher)

Interviews with pupils who had received additional literacy support across all three schools revealed that they held a range of responses to their schemes, from positive to negative:

Some of my mates call me names; sometimes they get jealous – some think it is good and the others just think I'm thick.
(Year 4 pupil)

In contrast, staff within the three schools generally perceived that pupils enjoyed participating in schemes.

Pupils' negative responses to additional literacy support were often related to the implications of being withdrawn from class for sessions. For example, some children experienced negative reactions from their class peers. This was a notable problem in schools where very specific and small groups of pupils were targeted and it also appeared to be more of an issue for older children than younger ones. Although staff and adult supporters recognised that this could be a problem, few of them perceived it as a real issue for children. One exception was a SENCO at one school, who stated:

One of the reasons we start with Year 3, [is] because by Year 6 they don't like being singled out for special treatment.

In addition, because the withdrawal of pupils from class was often at a time that was convenient to the additional literacy supporter, rather than to the child or the teacher, this meant that children missed out on what was being done in class and on occasion had to leave lessons and tasks midway. This proved unpopular with the children and some staff recognised that it could have an adverse effect on their attitudes towards additional literacy support if it meant that they had to forfeit tasks that they enjoyed:

Sometimes you have to miss out on fun things in class to go and read. (Year 5 pupil)

You can kill reading by saying to a child 'Stop what you are doing because you have to go and read now'; you'd turn it into a chore.
(class teacher)

Another limitation for pupils of using additional literacy supporters was that the schemes were totally dependent on the recruitment and commitment of the volunteers. This inevitably meant that it was not possible to provide all children with the opportunity to benefit and, given the current preoccupation with boys and literacy, some teachers felt that there was a danger that the needs of girls could easily be overlooked. In addition, it also meant that if volunteers were not committed and failed to attend sessions, or dropped out altogether, this could have adverse effects on pupils, who would sometimes feel that it was their fault:

> *The biggest problem is people who come for a couple of weeks and never come again. It's very upsetting for the children, you know. They're told that they're going to have this support and then it's almost like they don't like them or something when they haven't turned up.* (headteacher)

Although staff within two of the case study schools attempted to recruit male literacy supporters to act as positive role models, due to the relatively low number of male supporters that had volunteered to take part in schemes, staff were unable to assess the significance of their impact.

Parents: involvement and perceptions

Across all three schools, the parents of pupils selected for participation in the schemes were informed through letters and newsletters. These generally emphasised the benefits of the schemes for the pupils and, in the case of Callaghan Primary, provided parents with the opportunity to object to their child's participation (see Appendix 5.1 for a copy of the letter). Staff at one school considered it especially important to inform and involve parents so they could help to motivate pupils:

> *We informed parents about what we wanted to do with their children. We didn't say that they were underachieving or anything like that – what we said was that one thought they could do a bit better with a bit more support with their reading* (class teacher).

Staff within all of the case study schools generally considered it important to keep parents fully informed about, and involved with, their child's progress in the scheme. This was often achieved through letters (see Appendix 5.2), newsletters and informal feedback sessions to which parents were invited (see Appendix 5.3).

Across schools, staff noted that because schemes had only recently been implemented, they had not had much of a chance to obtain feedback from parents. In general, however, staff at all schools perceived that the parents of pupils receiving adult support were generally enthusiastic about the schemes and *'welcomed the fact that we were trying to help their boys'* (class teacher), which they felt was of benefit to their children. One parent stated:

> *My son thoroughly enjoyed it. Now he's a lot more competent and he's come on an awful lot.*

5.6 Evaluating the effectiveness of additional literacy supporters

All three of the primary schools monitored the impact of their use of additional literacy support on pupils, through reading tests. The reading scores at two of the schools showed that pupils who had received additional literacy support had made gains in terms of their reading scores. At the third school, monitoring systems had not been in place long enough for staff to assess the impact of additional literacy supporters on pupils' reading scores. At all three schools, it was too early for staff to assess whether gains made in reading scores were sustained by pupils after their participation in schemes. Illustration 5.2 below highlights the monitoring process adopted by one school to evaluate the impact of additional literacy supporters on pupils.

Illustration 5.2: **How one school monitored the impact of additional literacy supporters**

At Callaghan Primary, reading tests were done methodically before and after a pupil participated on the five- to six-week scheme and were repeated at a later date to assess whether gains made in pupils' reading scores had been sustained. At the time of this study, two blocks of sessions had been completed. The pupils' results are presented in Appendix 5.4 and reveal that the average gain made for all participating pupils was 0.7 years (just over eight months) in terms of reading age.

Two of the schools also used more qualitative approaches such as termly/half-termly discussions with class teachers, literacy supporters and parents to obtain feedback on the effects of using additional literacy supporters, and these, to date, have been positive.

Further evidence of the success of additional literacy supporters has been published in the VRH scheme annual report for 1997 – 98. The report presents the findings of an independent evaluation of the use of its helpers who work within primary schools across England. It stated:

Overall, children gained 10 months reading age after 8 months support. The 'moderately achieving' group of children, who were on average 18 months behind with their reading, showed the greatest gains – 12.5 months over 8 months. Boys also made better than average progress. All the children gained in confidence and developed a more positive attitude to reading (VRH, 1998, p. 4).

Similarly, in the evaluation Reading Partners (Tower Hamlets EBP, 1998), it was noted that after half a term of support from a volunteer helper there was a noticeable improvement in reading skills where: 72 per cent of pupils improved their intonation, expression and comprehension; 60 per cent improved their communication skills; and 50 per cent felt that they had significantly increased their level of motivation.

Future changes

Two of the schools intended to continue using additional literacy support in the future as long as they were able to recruit volunteers. Staff at one of these schools stated that in an attempt to encourage parents to volunteer, they were considering ways of launching the strategy more explicitly at the beginning of each term so that parents were made more aware of its existence and of the possible role that they could play. Staff at this school were also considering ways of providing supporters with training on a rolling basis so that new recruits could be catered for and long-term supporters provided with the necessary development. The third school also intended to continue using the strategy but staff were considering ways of incorporating it into the Literacy Hour.

5.7 Summary

This chapter has highlighted the way in which three primary schools used additional literacy support to address pupils' (predominantly boys') underachievement in literacy and thus gender gaps in performance. A summary of the main findings is presented below and a description of how one of the case study schools used additional literacy support is provided in Appendix 5.5.

Rationale

◆ Schools decided to tackle the issue of gender differences in achievement because they were aware that boys were underachieving compared to girls, especially in terms of literacy at the primary level, both nationally and within their own schools. Additional literacy support was adopted because the one-to-one support which it offered allowed the emphasis to be on the enjoyment of reading. This helped to improve pupils' attitudes, confidence and motivation regarding literacy. It was hoped that this would impact positively on pupil achievement, thus addressing gender gaps in performance.

The use of additional literacy supporters

◆ In general, additional literacy supporters worked with pupils for half a term. They usually went into schools at a regular time each week and worked with pupils on a one-to-one basis for roughly 20 minutes during lesson time. The main role of the additional literacy supporter was to increase pupils' levels of interest and motivation for reading by providing them with the opportunity to read material that was of interest to the pupil and by discussing what had been read.

- ◆ Schools often targeted pupils who were underachieving in literacy, either academically or socially (in terms of communication skills), for their age – the majority of whom tended to be boys. To identify these pupils, teachers used a combination of reading test results and professional judgement.

- ◆ Additional literacy supporters were usually provided with some form of training either within the school or through the organisation that had recruited them. Training usually included basic advice on possible strategies for supporting the literacy development of children.

- ◆ In terms of practical preparations, schools had to find space in which sessions could be held and had to obtain reading materials that were particularly aimed at boy/reluctant readers.

Key participants

- ◆ The main role of class teachers was to identify pupils for participation in schemes and to facilitate the withdrawal of pupils from class. Although class teachers were initially hesitant about the use of additional literacy supporters, over time they became convinced of the benefits for pupils and appreciated the fact that literacy supporters took the pressure off class teachers to ensure that the literacy needs of all pupils were being adequately met.

- ◆ Additional literacy supporters were recruited from a wide range of sources, from national organisations to pupils' family members. They usually made a commitment to schemes for various numbers of half-termly blocks. Participation in the schemes provided them with the opportunity to support the education of children and enabled them to develop greater community awareness.

- ◆ Schools adopted a variety of different approaches in terms of the way in which they informed children about their participation in schemes, in order to prevent any negative reactions. Pupils held a wide range of reactions to their schemes.

- ◆ Parents were mostly kept fully informed and involved in their child's participation in the scheme and their perceptions of the schemes were usually positive.

Impact on pupils

- ◆ The use of additional literacy supporters was considered beneficial for pupils because the one-to-one relationship provided an environment in which pupils could improve their attitudes and motivation towards literacy and thus their confidence and abilities in reading. It was felt that this led to greater pupil participation within class and impacted positively on their levels of achievement in other subject areas.

♦ The main limitations of using additional literacy supporters included finding space to hold sessions, the difficulties associated with withdrawing pupils from class and the fact that the success of schemes was dependent on the recruitment and commitment of the volunteers.

Evaluation of schemes

♦ The impact of using additional literacy supporters was generally monitored through the use of reading tests. Initial results indicated that pupils targeted had made gains in terms of their reading scores. However, it was too early to assess whether these gains were consistent or sustainable over time.

♦ Feedback from key participants suggested that the use of additional literacy supporters was having a positive effect on pupil achievement and thus on gender differences in performance.

Summarising, the following list highlights the main factors which staff stated were essential to ensure the success of utilising additional literacy supporters.

KEY FACTORS THAT MAKE ADDITIONAL LITERACY SUPPORT SUCCESSFUL

- **books are available which target reluctant (and) boy readers;**
- **adult volunteers are committed and provided with appropriate training;**
- **targeted pupils felt special and not stigmatised; and**
- **communication levels between all key participants are high.**

6. SUMMARY AND CONCLUSION

6.1 Summary of findings

The main findings from the previous three chapters regarding the use of mentoring, single-sex classes and additional literacy support to address gender differences in achievement are summarised below in terms of their main advantages and disadvantages.

Single-sex classes

Advantages for staff:

♦ Single-sex classes have raised staff awareness of gender gaps in performance.

♦ They have provided staff with the opportunity to focus more specifically on their teaching styles and relate their teaching methods and curriculum materials more precisely to the gender of the class.

Advantages for boys:

♦ Boy-friendly teaching strategies helped boys to find lessons more interesting and enjoyable.

♦ The use of competition worked to increase boys' levels of motivation.

♦ The use of male subject teachers as role models improved boys' perceptions of the value of learning some subjects that are stereotyped as 'feminine'.

♦ Single-sex classes helped to improve the relationship between teachers and boys, as the boys felt that they were valued and received more attention when girls were not present.

♦ The all-male environment increased the confidence of boys to contribute to lessons in general and in non-gender specific ways.

♦ The lack of girls in the class reduced boys' levels of distraction.

♦ In some cases, boys were better behaved because they were more interested and under less pressure to perform as there were no girls to impress.

Advantages for girls:

♦ The girls received more teacher attention because teachers did not have to spend time managing the behaviour of boys.

♦ Single-sex classes provided girls with more confidence to take part in lessons.

Disadvantages for staff:

♦ Some staff stated ideological concerns about teaching single-sex classes in terms of the social implications for pupils and the rationale for adopting them.

♦ Staff preferred to teach mixed-gender groups.

♦ Some staff were reluctant to teach all-boy (especially low-ability) classes because they felt that they were demanding in terms of behaviour management.

♦ The impact that single-sex classes had on setting procedures meant that classes had a wider range of ability and were often uneven in size, meaning that teachers had to differentiate more and use a wider range of materials.

Disadvantages for pupils:

♦ Single-sex classes meant that pupils missed out on the opportunity to gain the perspective of the opposite sex. This was considered to be particularly detrimental in English lessons.

♦ Some of the pupils stated that they missed not having the opposite sex in class.

♦ Only certain targeted pupils had the opportunity to experience single-sex classes rather than the whole year group.

Mentoring

Advantages for staff:

♦ It helped to improve teacher – pupil relations.

Advantages for pupils:

♦ Mentoring improved pupils' skills by providing them with extra support and tuition on how to organise their work and time effectively.

♦ It enabled pupils to feel that someone cared specifically for them.

♦ It increased pupils' levels of confidence, self-esteem, motivation and attitudes towards school and learning.

♦ Mentoring helped to challenge some boys' stereotypical anti-school and anti-learning attitudes.

♦ It encouraged pupils to take responsibility for their learning.

♦ It helped pupils to think about their post-16 future.

♦ Mentoring helped to improve pupils' levels of achievement.

Disadvantages for staff:

♦ Time was a major drawback for staff in terms of: finding an appropriate time within which to conduct mentoring sessions – either within or outside of lesson time; finding time to train mentors.

♦ Some staff felt that the training and support they received was not sufficient, which they felt resulted in pupils being offered differing qualities of mentoring.

♦ Some staff were not given a choice in who they mentored.

♦ Some staff mentored on a voluntary basis – i.e. in their own time and without pay.

♦ Employer – mentors were difficult to recruit and retain.

Disadvantages for pupils:

♦ Sessions were neither frequent enough nor long enough.

♦ Due to time limitations, pupils did not always get the opportunity to express themselves.

♦ Most pupils did not have any choice in who became their mentor.

♦ If mentors dropped out, this sometimes had an adverse effect on the pupil.

♦ The identification of pupils for participation in the scheme was not always accurate.

♦ Some pupils experienced negative peer pressure for participating in mentoring schemes.

♦ Participation in some schemes was voluntary, which meant that some targeted pupils preferred not to participate or dropped out.

♦ Not all pupils, in all schools, were able to be mentored.

Additional literacy support

Advantages in general:

♦ The use of additional literacy supporters enabled schools to make important links with the wider community.

Advantages for staff:

♦ The use of ALS did not increase the workload of class teachers.

♦ The use of ALS helped to take the pressure off class teachers to ensure that the needs of all pupils were effectively met in terms of the levels of support and attention that they required to improve their levels of literacy.

Advantages for additional literacy supporters

♦ Sessions could be scheduled to take place at a time that was most convenient for volunteers.

♦ They were provided with an opportunity to gain insight into how schools worked.

♦ Additional literacy support provided them with an opportunity to be of service to local schools.

Advantages for pupils:

♦ They received one-to-one support for concentrated periods which they would not otherwise experience.

♦ Pupils were encouraged to recognise that reading can be enjoyable.

♦ Additional literacy support enabled pupils to improve their self-esteem and confidence in literacy as well as their attitudes towards reading.

♦ Improvements in pupils' literacy levels had positive effects on their achievement in other subject areas and on their behaviour.

♦ The use of male role models helped some boys to improve their perceptions of literacy.

Disadvantages in general

♦ Additional literacy support schemes often relied solely on the ability of project coordinators to recruit and retain committed volunteers.

♦ If supporters were not committed to schemes, this could be disruptive to staff and have adverse effects on pupils.

♦ It was often difficult to find space within which to hold sessions.

Disadvantages for staff:

♦ Class teachers had to ensure that pupils did not miss out on anything vital when they were withdrawn from class for sessions and, if they did, were given the chance to catch up.

Disadvantages for pupils:

♦ Sessions took place during lesson time, which meant that pupils sometimes missed out on important and interesting topics.

♦ Schools were not able to provide all pupils with additional literacy support.

♦ Some pupils felt stigmatised because they were withdrawn from lessons for additional literacy support.

6.2 Discussion

The main aims of this project were to explore the range of strategies currently operating in schools to address gender differences in achievement and to investigate the impact of a sample of these strategies. In addition, it was intended that the findings would provide useful guidance to LEAs and schools.

Phase 1 of this study provided an overview of the main issues regarding gender differences in achievement through a review of relevant research literature and an insight into the ways in which schools were currently responding to the issue of girls' outperformance of boys. Phase 2 of the study, upon which this report is based, investigated the way in which three strategies – single-sex classes, mentoring and additional literacy support – were adopted and implemented within a number of case study schools. This conclusion attempts to pull the findings together in order to provide a general framework for teachers, LEA advisers and researchers interested in developing further strategies for addressing gender differences in achievement.

The findings from this report suggest that there are four main areas which need to be carefully considered when introducing strategies for addressing gender differences in achievement.

6.2. 1. Equal opportunities

It is important to identify where gender gaps in performance are actually occurring. Schools generally used a range of performance data to analyse where gender differences were in terms of pupil gender, pupil ability and subject area. As a result, the pupils who were most frequently targeted tended to be boys who were underachieving at specific points (such as the C/D GCSE grade borderline or the five or more A – C GCSE borderline). Schools adopted this approach and focused on those pupils, arguably because a rise in performance at these levels would lead to an increase in overall performance levels for the school. The overall improvement of five or more A – C grades would then enhance the school's position in the league tables. In other words, the criterion for increasing achievement was closely linked to political pressures rather than necessarily targeting pupils who were underachieving to the greatest extent. Although this focus on borderline pupils at the end of key stages was not apparent within the primary schools that participated in this study, it is an issue at both the primary and secondary level given the importance now accorded to pupil attainment at the end of each key stage.

Staff within many schools recognised this pressure and therefore made a conscious effort to ensure that some degree of equality of opportunity existed. This was achieved, for example, by focusing on both boys and girls who met the criteria by which they defined 'underachievement' and by focusing on pupils who were underachieving in social as well as academic terms.

6.2.2. School issues

It is important to choose strategies that are appropriate and most likely to succeed within each *individual* school. To achieve this, staff in the case study schools often conducted preliminary research in order to identify where gender differences were prevalent within their school and the strategies that could be adopted to address these differences. It was important to take into consideration the local context and the ethos of the school when deciding on which strategy to adopt. Within some schools, existing strategies were modified in order to focus on the new issue of gender differences. For example, within one school, mentoring had been used as a method of raising achievement *per se*, but, once staff became aware that there was a significant gender gap in performance, the use of mentoring was redirected to a more specific target, namely underachieving boys.

In addition, there was a general awareness among staff that strategies ought to be reviewed regularly and, if necessary, modified in relation to national and local changes and in terms of the different needs of new cohorts and variations in staffing. As a result, once strategies were adopted, they were continually in a state of evolution, being modified in light of the results of evaluations and changing circumstances. This reveals that staff were usually aware that any strategies adopted were not 'quick-fix' or ultimate solutions to complex problems but represented practical and feasible ways of tackling issues as they arose.

However, there was a sense among some staff that once strategies were working effectively, the basic tenets on which they were based (such as the use of different teaching styles for boys and girls) ought to become embedded within the culture of the school so that 'good practice' could be extended throughout the school.

6.2.3. Effects of strategies

It is important, when deciding on the strategy to adopt, to have a clear understanding of how it might work in school. Within the research literature it is possible to identify two main strands of explanation for girls' outperformance of boys. Firstly, it has been suggested that there are variations in pupils' learning styles which require different teaching methods in order for pupils to fulfil their potential. And secondly, it is claimed that there are variations in pupils' orientation towards school and learning which mean that some pupils find it easier to succeed within the education system.

The different strategies adopted within the case study schools tended to provide staff with the opportunity to tackle both of these causes simultaneously. For example, single-sex classes enabled staff to provide all-boy and all-girl classes with teaching styles and curriculum materials that were most appropriate to their learning styles whilst providing pupils with an environment which encouraged them to value learning and achievement. Similarly, mentoring programmes allowed staff to tackle the specific weaknesses that are often associated with the learning styles of boys and girls and also the opportunity to tackle individual problems in terms of perceptions and attitudes.

Although strategies such as these provide staff with the opportunity to address the possible causes of gender gaps in performance, they do have a number of implications. Firstly, there is a danger that staff will be encouraged to exploit the differing areas of male and female strengths, rather than address their weaknesses, in an attempt to improve levels of achievement. This may actually have the undesired effect of reinforcing gender stereotypes. For example, the use of certain male-orientated texts to improve boys' levels of literacy may reinforce their preference for particular reading and writing styles. Similarly, the use of male role models to challenge boys' stereotypical perceptions of the 'femininity' of certain subjects may serve to undermine the authority of female teachers.

Secondly, given the current popular focus on boys rather than girls, there is a danger that staff will concentrate their efforts and resources into modifying the learning environment to address the needs of boys without necessarily making as much effort to address the needs of girls, simply because girls are achieving more than boys. As a result, girls do not appear to be provided with equal opportunities to fulfil their potential.

Thirdly, it is useful to recognise that the idea of modifying teaching approaches and educational environments to match the learning preferences of boys and girls is based on the rather simplistic notion that all boys and all girls have similar learning preferences. Whilst this might be accurate in general terms, it is important to recognise that the learning styles of boys and girls are not only influenced by their gender but may well be influenced by other factors such as their ability levels and individual characteristics.

Finally, it is important to appreciate the impact which the implementation of different strategies can have at the broader whole-school level in terms of factors such as pupil organisation and teacher role. For example, as stated previously, the implementation of single-sex classes inevitably has implications for pupil organisation in terms of the extent to which pupils can be grouped by ability.

Therefore when deciding on which strategy to adopt, staff do not only need to have a comprehensive understanding of: where gender differences in achievement are prevalent; which strategies are likely to succeed within the ethos of the school; and how these strategies will enable gender gaps in performance to be reduced. They also need to appreciate the impact that particular strategies can have on schools at a practical level (in terms of issues such as pupil organisation) and at a theoretical level (in terms of issues such as the effect of treating boys and girls differently on the ethos of a school).

6.2.4. Evaluation

It is important to implement some level of quantitative and qualitative evaluation in order to enable modifications to be made to the strategy for the following year and in order to gain some sense of the efficacy of the strategy. However, it can be difficult to evaluate the effectiveness of strategies given their continually changing nature, the impact of uncontrollable additional factors and because the implementation of a strategy will inevitably have some impact on the learning process, due to its novelty value.

In summary, for those who are considering implementing strategies to address gender differences in achievement, it is important to use a range of data to identify where gender gaps in achievement are prevalent, at both the academic and social level, and which groups of pupils appear to be underachieving, in terms of gender, ability level and possibly other social characteristics such as social class and race. The choice of strategy needs to be made in relation to the identified problem as well as the school context and ethos. The implementation of strategies also needs to be conducted in an experimental way with the full commitment of staff. Finally, strategies need to be carefully monitored and evaluated so that they can be continually modified in relation to the changing circumstance within schools and the national climate.

6.3 Future research

The findings from this report reveal a need for further research into the efficacy of different strategies for addressing gender differences in achievement. It has been shown that staff within the case study schools have experienced a number of problems with evaluating the effects of different interventions. It would therefore be useful if researchers in the future were able to conduct large-scale studies into the use of different strategies for addressing gender differences in achievement. This would enable multilevel techniques to be used in order to control various factors and thus detect how significant the impact of different strategies was on pupil achievement.

Such research would also need to investigate the processes by which different strategies impact on gender gaps in performance so that there can be greater clarification as to the possible causes of these variations and thus more accurate suggestions for possible solutions – something which was beyond the remit of this project.

In order to gain a more comprehensive understanding of gender differences – in terms of its extent, its possible causes and thus the types of strategies which could be adopted to address it – it would be useful if future research adopted a more complex approach. This could be achieved by investigating the impact of different strategies in relation to pupils' multiple social characteristics (such as their class, race, ability and age in addition to their gender) and the different local contexts within which schools are based.

Finally, it is important for future research to investigate the impact of effective strategies for addressing gender differences at a broader social level. This is because the findings from this study suggest that external political pressure is encouraging schools to concentrate on addressing 'underachievement' according to a narrow definition (the number of five or more A – Cs at GCSE), which may result in the implementation of strategies which are highly effective in terms of addressing gender gaps in performance but which may actually have a detrimental impact on issues of equal opportunity as well as on pupils' wider experiences of schooling and learning.

REFERENCES

ARNOLD, R. (1997). *Raising Levels of Achievement in Boys.* Slough: NFER, EMIE.

ARNOT, M., GRAY, J., JAMES, M., RUDDUCK. J. and DUVEEN, G. (1998). *Recent Research on Gender and Educational Performance* (OFSTED Reviews of Research). London: The Stationery Office.

BEATTIE, A. and HOLDEN, R. (1994). 'Young person mentoring in schools: the Doncaster experience', *Education + Training* (Special Issue: Young Person Mentoring), **36**, 5, 8-15.

BELL, J.F. (1990). 'A brief review of national comparisons of performance of pupils attending single-sex and co-educational English schools', *Education Section Review - British Psychological Society*, **14**, 2, 32-6.

BLEACH, K. (1998a). 'Introduction.' In: BLEACH, K. (Ed) *Raising Boys' Achievement in Schools.* Stoke-on-Trent: Trentham Books.

BLEACH, K. (1998b). 'Why the likely lads lag behind.' In: BLEACH, K. (Ed) *Raising Boys' Achievement in Schools.* Stoke-on-Trent: Trentham Books.

BRAY, R., GARDNER, C., PARSONS, N., DOWNES, P. and HANNAN, G. (1997). *Can Boys Do Better?* Leicester: Secondary Heads Association.

CARVEL, J. (1997). 'Girls outclassing boys', *Guardian*, 26 November, 1.

CASSIDY, S. (1999). 'Gender gap widens to a gulf', *Times Educ. Suppl.*, **4309**, 29 January, 6.

CAUDREY, A. (1985). 'Growing role of parents in class causes alarm', *Times Educ. Suppl.*, **3589**, 1, 12 April.

CLUTTERBUCK, D. (1991). *Everyone Needs a Mentor: Fostering Talent at Work.* London: Institute of Personnel Management.

COHEN, M. (1998). 'A habit of healthy idleness: boys' underachievement in historical perspective.' In: EPSTEIN, D., ELWOOD, J., HEY, V. and MAW, J. (Eds) *Failing Boys? Issues in Gender and Achievement.* Buckingham: Open University Press.

CRUMP, S.J. (1990). 'Gender and curriculum: power and being female', *British Journal of Sociology of Education*, **11**, 4, 365-85.

DALE, R.R. (1969). *Mixed or Single-sex School? Volume 1: a Research Study about Pupil – Teacher Relationships.* London: Routledge & Kegan Paul.

DALE, R.R. (1971). *Mixed or Single-sex School? Volume 2: Some Social Aspects.* London: Routledge & Kegan Paul.

DALE, R.R. (1974). *Mixed or Single-sex School? Volume 3: Attainment, Attitudes and Overview.* London: Routledge & Kegan Paul.

DALY, P. (1996). 'The effects of single-sex and coeducational schooling on girls' achievement', *Research Papers in Education*, **11**, 3, 289-306.

DEAN, C. (1998). 'Failing boys "public burden number one"', *Times Educ. Suppl.*, **4300**, 27 November, 1.

EPSTEIN D., ELWOOD, J., HEY, V. and MAW, J. (1998). 'Schoolboy frictions: feminism and "failing" boys.' In: EPSTEIN, D., ELWOOD, J., HEY, V. and MAW, J. (Eds) *Failing Boys? Issues in Gender and Achievement.* Buckingham: Open University Press.

FAULKNER, J. (1991). 'Mixed-sex schooling and equal opportunity for girls: a contradiction in terms?' *Research Papers in Education*, **6**, 3, 197-223.

FISHER, J. (1994). 'The case for girls-only schools', *Education Review*, **8**, 2, 49-50.

GALLAGHER, A.M. (1997). *Educational Achievement and Gender: a Review of Research Evidence on the Apparent Underachievement of Boys* (DENI Research Report No. 6). Bangor: DENI.

GAY, B. (1994). 'What is mentoring?' *Education + Training* (Special Issue: Young Person Mentoring), **36**, 5, 4-7.

GOLDEN, S. and SIMS, D. (1997). *Review of Industrial Mentoring in Schools.* Slough: NFER.

GREAT BRITAIN. DEPARTMENT FOR EDUCATION AND EMPLOYMENT (1997). *The Implementation of the National Literacy Strategy.* London: DFEE.

HIROM, K. and MITCHELL, G. (1999). 'The effect of mentoring on the academic achievement of boys'. Paper presented at the British Educational Research Association Conference, University of Sussex, Brighton, 2-5 September.

HUGILL, B. (1998). 'The male liberator's sit-down protest', *Times Educ. Suppl.*, **4296**, 30 October, 11.

HYLAN, I. and POSTLETHWAITE, K. (1997). '*Mentoring: does it work?*' *Managing Schools Today*, **7**, 1, 26-7, 29.

KENWAY, J. (1995). 'Masculinities in schools: under siege, on the defensive and under reconstruction?' *Discourse*, **16**, 1, 59-79.

KERRY, T. (1998). '*Mentoring: can it help the SENCO?*' *Special Children*, **109**, 17-19.

MacDONALD, A., SAUNDERS, L. and BENEFIELD, P. (1999). *Boys' Achievement, Progress, Motivation and Participation: Issues Raised by the Recent Literature.* Slough: NFER.

McNALLY, J. (1994). 'Students, schools and a matter of mentors', *International Journal of Educational Management*, **8**, 5, 18-23.

MAHONY, P. (1985). *Schools for the Boys? Co-education Reassessed.* London: Hutchinson. Cited in: FAULKNER, J. (1991). 'Mixed-sex schooling and equal opportunity for girls: a contradiction in terms?' *Research Papers in Education,* **6**, 3, 197-223.

MAHONY, P. (1998). 'Girls will be girls and boys will be first.' In: EPSTEIN, D., ELWOOD, J., HEY, V. and MAW, J. (Eds) *Failing Boys? Issues in Gender and Achievement.* Buckingham: Open University Press.

MARJORAM, T. (1994). 'Are/should boys and girls gifted in mathematics be taught together?' *Gifted Education International,* **9**, 3, 152-3.

MEASOR, L., TIFFIN, C. and FRY, K. (1996). 'Gender and sex education: a study of adolescent responses', *Gender and Education,* **8**, 3, 275-88.

MERRIAM, S. (1983). 'Mentors and protégés: a critical review of the literature', *Adult Education Quarterly,* **33**, 3, 161-73.

MONAGHAN, J. (1992). 'Mentoring: person, process, practice and problems', *British Journal of Educational Studies,* **40**, 3, 248-63.

MURPHY, P. and ELWOOD, J. (1996). 'Gendered experiences, choices and achievement – exploring the links.' Paper presented at the 23rd Annual IAEA Conference 'Equity Issues in Education and Assessment', Durban, South Africa, 9-13 June.

MURPHY, P. and ELWOOD, J. (1998). 'Gendered learning outside and inside school: influences on achievement.' In: EPSTEIN, D., ELWOOD, J., HEY, V. and

MAW, J. (Eds) *Failing Boys? Issues in Gender and Achievement.* Buckingham: Open University Press.

NOBLE, C. (1998). 'Helping boys do better in their primary schools.' In: BLEACH, K. (Ed) *Raising Boys' Achievement in Schools.* Stoke on Trent: Trentham Books.

NORTHERN EXAMINATIONS AND ASSESSMENT BOARD (1996). 'Gender differences in the GCSE', *NEAB Standard,* Summer, 6-7.

OFFICE FOR STANDARDS IN EDUCATION and EQUAL OPPORTUNITIES COMMISSION (1996). *The Gender Divide: Performance Differences between Boys and Girls at School.* London: HMSO.

PICKERING, J. (1997). *Raising Boys' Achievement* (The School Effectiveness Series). Stafford: Network Educational Press.

PIMENOFF, S. (1995). 'Gender on the agenda?' *Report,* **17**, 4, 10-11.

QUALIFICATIONS AND CURRICULUM AUTHORITY (1998). *Can do Better: Raising Boys' Achievement in English.* London: QCA.

RAPHAEL REED, L. (1998). 'Zero tolerance: gender performance and school failure.' In: EPSTEIN, D., ELWOOD, J., HEY, V. and MAW, J. (Eds) *Failing Boys? Issues in Gender and Achievement.* Buckingham: Open University Press.

ROBINSON, P. and SMITHERS, A. (1999). 'Should the sexes be separated for secondary education – comparisons of single-sex and co-educational schools?' *Research Papers in Education*, **14**, 1, 23-49.

ROWE, K. (1988). 'Single-sex and mixed-sex classes: the effects of class type on student achievement, confidence and participation in mathematics', *Australian Journal of Education,* **32**, 2, 180-202.

SMITHERS, A. and ROBINSON, P. (1995). *Co-educational and Single-sex Schooling: Interim Report.* Manchester: University of Manchester, School of Education, Centre for Education and Employment.

STABLES, A. (1990). 'Differences between pupils from mixed and single-sex schools in their enjoyment of school subjects and in their attitudes to science and to school', *Educational Review*, **42**, 3, 221-30.

STEEDMAN, J. (1984). *Examination Results in Mixed and Single-sex Schools: Findings from The National Child Development Study.* Manchester: Equal Opportunities Commission. Cited in: STEEDMAN, J. (1985). 'Examination results in mixed and single-sex secondary schools.' In: REYNOLDS, D. (Ed) *Studying School Effectiveness.* London: Falmer Press.

STEEDMAN, J. (1985). 'Examination results in mixed and single-sex secondary schools.' In: REYNOLDS, D. (Ed) *Studying School Effectiveness.* London: Falmer Press.

STRAND, S. (1999). 'Ethnic group, sex and economic disadvantage: associations with pupils' educational progress from baseline to the end of key stage 1', *British Educational Research Journal*, **25**, 2, 179-202.

SUKHNANDAN, L. (1999). *An Investigation into Gender Differences in Achievement. Phase 1: a Review of Recent Research and LEA Information on Provision.* Slough: NFER.

TOPPING, K. (1986). *Parents as Educators: Teaching Parents to Teach their Children.* London: Croom Helm.

TOWER HAMLETS EDUCATION BUSINESS PARTNERSHIP (1998) Reading Partners 1997/1998 Evaluation. Unpublished report.

VOLUNTEER READING HELP (1998). *Volunteer Reading Help Annual Report 1997-1998.* London: Volunteer Reading Help.

WARRINGTON, M. and YOUNGER, M. (1997). 'Gender and achievement: the debate at GCSE', *Education Review*, **10**, 1, 21–7.

WILTSHIRE EDUCATION SUPPORT & TRAINING (1996). *Boys & English: Discussion Documents, INSET Materials and an Account of Development Work in Three Wiltshire Schools.* Trowbridge: WEST.

WOODD, M. (1997). 'Gender differences in mentoring: a biographical reflection', *Educational Management & Administration*, **25**, 1, 25-34.

APPENDICES

Appendix 1.1

Definition of 'good practice'

In the pro formas that were sent to LEAs, advisers were asked to nominate schools which they felt had successfully implemented strategies to address gender differences and therefore represented examples of 'good practice'. The following list of criteria was compiled to assist LEA advisers in identifying appropriate schools.

Schools nominated as examples of good practice should include:

1. schools that have taken a systematic approach in their identification of the problem and their decision to implement a particular strategy;

2. schools that have systems in place for monitoring outcomes or the strategies (e.g. systematic observation, tracking of pupils, tests, questionnaires);

3. schools that have evidence that the strategy is successfully addressing the issue.

Appendix 3.1

A letter sent to parents updating them on their child's progress in single-sex classes

To the parents of ....

Dear ....

I would like to inform you that we are **very pleased** with ....'s work on the GCSE English course. .... has shown exactly the right attitude to homework, classwork, behaviour and uniform.

Thank you for your support of ....'s work. If there is any comment you wish you make, please use the attached form.

Head of English

x ————————————————————————————
————————————————————

To:

I/We wish to make the following comments about the progress of our son
....
....
....
....
....

Appendix 3.2

Parent responses to information on their child's progress in single-sex classes

---

◆We wish to make the following comments about the progress of our son:

We are very pleased that [child] has settled down in English and that he is showing the right attitude to his work

We would like to thank [teacher] for your help and

Signed:_____(Parent/Guardian) support with

I/We wish to make the following comments about the progress of our son:

Thank you for letting us know how well [child] is doing in English. With your expert methods, he has never enjoyed the lessons as much as he has at

Signed:_____(Parent/Guardian)

I/We wish to make the following comments about the progress of our son:

I would like to thank you for letting us know how well you feel [child] is doing, I do get very concerned about his progress, As long as you are pleased with his efforts I feel reassured he is doing his best. His writing still causes problems and he must keep trying hard to improve it.

Signed:_____(Parent/Guardian)

Thankyou again for your support and encouragement.

Appendix 3.3

Pupil questionnaire for evaluating single-sex classes

Single-Sex Groups

Questions for one-to-one interviews with Year 10 students

1. How did you initially feel when you heard/were told that you were going to be taught in single-sex groups in English at GCSE?

    _____

    _____

    _____

    _____

    _____

2. What was the reaction of friends/other people in the year group?

    _____

    _____

    _____

    _____

    _____

3. Why do you think the English Faculty took the decision? Do you know what research has shown about boys and girls' achievements in English?

    _____

    _____

    _____

    _____

    _____

4. Do you feel that you were given an adequate explanation?

    _____

    _____

    _____

    _____

    _____

5. What do you like about working in a single-sex group?

    _____

    _____

    _____

    _____

    _____

6. What do you not like?

_____

_____

_____

_____

_____

7. Would you like to return to mixed groups next year? Why/Why not?

_____

_____

_____

_____

_____

8 Can you think of any other subject areas which might be better for you if you were taught as all boys/all girls? Which ones and why?

_____

_____

_____

_____

_____

_____

9 Do you feel you have made more progress/less progress/the same amount of progress as you would in mixed groups?

_____

_____

_____

_____

10 Do you feel that behaviour has been better or worse than in mixed-sex groups? Can you say why you think this?

_____

_____

_____

_____

_____

_____

_____

I 1. This year we deliberately made it that male teachers would teach the boys' groups and female teachers teach the girls' groups - What do you think of that? Do you think it makes a difference?

_____
_____
_____
_____
_____
_____

12. Do you feel more confident in talking aloud in class or reading out loud? If yes, why do you think this is? If no, what stops you?

_____
_____
_____
_____
_____

13. What grade do you expect to get in GCSE language next year?

_____
_____

14. How does this grade compare to what you expect to achieve in other subjects that you are studying?

_____
_____
_____
_____
_____

Finally, thank you very much for taking time to fill in this questionnaire. The purpose of it is so that we can see how effective this initiative has been this year and would like to assure you that your views expressed here will be taken into account and acted upon. If there is anything else that you would like to add about the initiative into single-sex groupings, feel free to add your comments below.

_____
_____
_____
_____
_____
_____
_____
_____

Appendix 3.4

Pupil responses to questionnaire evaluating single-sex classes

Evaluation of single-sex grouping arrangements in English (Year 10)

Aims
* Evaluate relative performance of boys and girls in English
* To see whether the differential disparity has decreased
* Collate perceptions of students and staff re. effectiveness of single-sex classes in terms of,
    - behaviour
    - attitude to work
    - academic progress and achievement
* To see whether there were any differences in boys' and girls' perceptions

Method
* Student questionnaire (30 students in Year 10, 15 boys and 15 girls, taken from different teaching groups)
* Staff responses to sheet asking for their perceptions of strengths and weaknesses of initiative

Student questionnaire
A blank copy of the questionnaire is included with this report. It was made clear to the students that honest opinions were sought after and anonymity was guaranteed. The only restriction on this was to code sheets so that I could identify the sex of the responder and the teaching group that they were in. Fourteen questions were asked in all; an analysis of the findings and a selection of responses from some of the questions are given below.

1. **How did you initially feel when you were told that you were going to be taught in single-sex groups in English at GCSE?**

    60% of students for the change (no difference between boys and girls)
    20% against
    20% not bothered

Student comments

"I felt that it was a bad idea because I wouldn't have the chance to work with my friends who I had worked with for 3 years" (Boy)

"I thought it would be alright because we would have no girls to show off to and then we will get our work done" (Boy)

"I felt alright about it. The only thing was there was not enough groups" (Boy)

"Shocked when I heard, thought it was a bad idea" (Girl)

"Surprised and excited also disappointed that we would not get to work with the boys" (Girl)

"I thought it would be a good idea because we could concentrate more, but I also enjoyed it with mixed classes as we would get a mixture of opinions" (Girl)

"I thought it would be good because girls distract me and I can work harder without them" (Boy)

"I thought it would be a good idea as if the boys were in competition with the girls" (Boy)

"I thought it would be good to see if the work rate would change" (Girl)

2. Do you feel that you were given an adequate explanation? 66% said yes, 33% said no

In general boys felt that they were given much greater explanation. This could well be because I used much of the INSET material I used for the staff presentation with my boys group. Next year it will be important to share research findings with students in a more controlled and detailed manner.

3. What do you like about working in a single-sex group?

"I like the fact that we can talk readily about the girls without being called sexist. Also we don't get distracted because they aren't with us" (Boy)

"..when boys write they find it hard to write a lot, whereas girls just waffle on and take away from the boys' efforts" (Boy)

"I think that with us all being boys, and having a male teacher, we all get on well socially and can have a laugh because we get on well with our teacher. When it is time to work we can" (Boy)

"You can express feelings more freely" (Boy)

"More confidence to speak in front of the class" (Girl)

"I like being able to discuss things with each other without boys becoming offensive. I also like the fact that the girls are more mature and don't act stupid when discussing things" (Girl)

"Nothing!" (Girl)

"It's easier to open up and express your views" (Girl)

"More people express their thoughts and know that they won't be laughed at if they get something wrong" (Girl)

In summary boys liked: talk more freely; more work completed; greater confidence; tasks geared more towards their strengths; no need to show off.

Girls liked: More confidence in speaking tasks; everyone gets on well; getting more teacher attention; less distraction; less intimidating atmosphere.

4. What do you not like?

"Sometimes I feel like I'm 'with the lads' and get carried away" (Boy)

"There's nothing I dislike about the new teaching groups because it works well and my English has improved vastly" (Boy)

"You can't talk to girls, you have to talk to a boy" (Boy)

"We don't get the boys' side of the argument and opinions on things. I also don't like the fact that when we read a play we don't get anyone to read out the male parts" (Girl)

"The bitchiness most girls have towards each other" (Girl)

"It's not that I don't like it, it's just a bit boring and old-fashioned" (Girl) sometimes boring the boys make us laugh"

"There's nothing that I don't like because it's now a lot more peaceful and everyone works better" (Girl)

5. Would you like to return to mixed groups next year?

30% said yes
57% said no
13% didn't know

Most 'yes' responses came from the top girls' group. Both boys groups wish to maintain existing arrangements.

6. Can you think of any other subject areas which might be better for you if you were taught as all boys/all girls? Which ones and why?

Just under 50% of those questioned felt other subjects could benefit. Comments included: "PSE because all the girls work well but the boys just muck around..." (Girl) "PE might be separated when particular sports are played" (Girl)

"I think Science should be a single-sex group because mainly the boys mess around and if the boys were taught together they might work harder" (Girl)

"We have a good environment in out textiles lessons as well as no boys chose textiles..." (Girl)

"I think Maths because in my class all the boys just mess around and I can't do my work. It is hard to concentrate with them jogging the table..." (Girl)

"R.E. Most of the boys are sent out and this disturbs us and sometimes we even have to forget practical lessons and copy out of a text book" (Girl)

"I think it should be done in the three main classes, Maths, Science, English, if they have proof it is better" (Boy)

"Science because boys do not answer when girls are around" (Boy)

"Languages is an area where girls are generally better than boys. We can prove this from the distribution in the top group. Out of a class of 25+ there are only 5 boys" (Boy)

"PSE because if we were studying sex education we could (if we had any problems) talk about them without feeling embarrassed" (Boy)

7. **Do you feel you have made more progress/less progress/the same amount of progress as you would in mixed groups?**

56% felt they were making more progress 4% felt they were making less progress
40% felt they were making the same progress

8. **Do you feel that behaviour has been better or worse than in mixed-sex groups? Can you say why you think this?**

76% felt behaviour was better 4% felt it was worse
20% felt it was the same

Comments included;

"I feel behaviour is pretty good. We do have our odd silly moments but they are quite rare" (Boy)

"Better, because in the boys it's mainly homework detentions are given for, whereas in mixed lads try to impress girls" (Boy)

"I think behaviour has been better because our teacher has been hard on us; he has made us do the work but at the same time we can have a laugh" (Boy)

"I think the behaviour is the same as in mixed-sex classes as people still give in homework late and misbehave in class" (Girl)

"Boys are a little less mature than girls so the behaviour has been better" (Girl)

"The behaviour is better because the girls can say things without the boys making stupid noises and stuff like that" (Girl)

"I think that the behaviour in a single-sex group has got better because they (the boys) have realised that you come to school to learn, not mess around" (Girl)

9. **Do you feel more confident in talking aloud in class or reading out loud? If yes, why do you think this is so? If no, what stops you?**

64% felt more confident 36% felt the same
0% felt less confident

Comments included;

"I do feet more confident. If the boys were here then if you went wrong some would laugh and make you feel uncomfortable" (Girl N-B. A no. of girls made similar observations)

"If we were mixed it would make me speak out more. It's more competitive with the boys" (Girl)

"I feel the same as I always have about talking and reading out loud. I have never liked it and don't think anything would change this" (Girl)

"Yes I do because there are no girls and if I get an answer wrong in front of them I would feel a bit silly" (Boy)

"Because boys of our age are always trying to impress the girls, they are very wary of what they say. With no girls in a group boys will say what they feet without being worried about looking silly" (Boy)

10. How does the grade you expect to achieve in English Language compare to what you expect to achieve in other subjects that you are studying?

16% thought it was higher 4% thought it was lower
60% thought it was the same 20% didn't know

Appendix 3.5

Teacher responses to an evaluation of single-sex classes

The perceptions of the English Faculty

Strengths
* Confidence building, especially in speaking exercises. The girls are very eager and willing to answer and ask questions in class

* There is a very good class atmosphere. Group work is excellent because of good relationships

* The girls are very competitive with each other- and also eager to 'bear the boys' groups with their results

* The girls work at a fairly similar pace. They do not rush through things - reflecting is very strong

* Boys more confident and are able to empathise more

* Material can be geared more towards needs and interests

* Objective view of sexism (eventually!)

* Raises expectations (competition with girls' groups)

* Fewer instances of poor behaviour in the classrooms and around the Faculty area

* Boys, especially in the top group, much more positive about English. Increase in esteem- can 'do' English and can articulate feelings and emotional response. Quality of S+L work often staggeringly high

* As HoF I have received only 2 blue referral forms ALL YEAR!

Weaknesses
* Only two boys' groups as opposed to three for girls - less flexibility in setting leading to a large and consequently challenging lower boys group

* Boys' groups need to be monitored carefully by teachers to ensure a 'laddish' culture does not develop

* I suspect that the key determining feature may well be the effectiveness of the individual teacher

* Problems when cover needed (ownership of room and teacher perceived by group)

* Some students tend to 'hang around' outside the classrooms in the English area- the girls are often reluctant to begin a lesson as it means tearing themselves away from the lads

* Whilst have confidence that GCSE results will improve for both boys and girls, think that differential disparity will increase!

Limitations of research
*Student sample rather small *Vested interest of evaluator! *Limited data collection techniques; much of evidence anecdotal

*Difficulty of quantifying progress made. Long time-scale before see whether initiative achieves its aims

Appendix 3.6

A case study summary of a school that had implemented single-sex classes

Greengage School was based in the suburbs of a city in the north of England. It was an 11 – 16 school which served a predominantly middle-class population. Almost a quarter of the school's population were from ethnic minority backgrounds. A few years ago, the deputy head intuitively felt that middle-ability boys in key stage 4 were failing to fulfil their potential. She therefore decided to analyse statistical data on pupil performance and teachers' predictions of pupils' GCSE grades. This analysis confirmed her suspicions so she decided to instigate a whole-school initiative into raising boys' levels of achievement, in which individual departments were given responsibility for addressing the issue within their own subject area.

Within the mathematics department, staff had a brainstorming session about what they could do. They looked at the set placement of the Year 11 boys identified as underachieving by the deputy head and found that they were all in the two middle sets of the six-set system. Staff therefore decided to implement single-sex classes, on a trial basis, in an attempt to improve the performance of this target group.

Few practical preparations had to be made in order to organise pupils into single-sex classes, as all of the pupils in Year 11 were block-timetabled for mathematics. Staff therefore simply combined the two middle-ability sets and divided them according to gender rather than ability, so that there was one middle-ability all-boy class and one middle-ability all-girl class. Once the decision was made, staff presented the idea to the pupils who would be affected, and to their parents, as fully and as positively as possible. In general, both pupils and parents greeted the idea with enthusiasm. Staff were given a limited amount of training through an INSET day, although there was a sense that staff would increasingly modify their teaching approaches, as necessary, as their experience of teaching single-sex classes grew.

At the end of the first year, the evaluation of single-sex classes revealed that they had worked effectively so it was decided to extend their use to the intermediate sets of Year 10 as well as Year 11. However, some staff within the department expressed concern about teaching either just an all-boy or just an all-girl class. In response a carousel system was introduced which meant that the two teachers (one of whom was male and one of whom was female) taking the single-sex classes in each year group alternated between classes, teaching the same topics to both. An added advantage of introducing this system was that evaluations of single-sex classes did not have to take into consideration the impact of different teachers on pupils' experiences of learning.

Staff at the school evaluated the impact of single-sex classes through discussions with teachers, pupils and parents, and in terms of pupil attainment, primarily GCSE results. The findings from evaluations of the first year showed that teachers, pupils and parents generally perceived single-sex classes as beneficial, particularly for the boys. In addition, the overall number of boys achieving A – C grades in GCSE mathematics for that year increased from 49 per cent (in the previous year) to 60 per cent.

Staff felt that the strategy was successful because it had been presented to the pupils in a positive, collaborative way and because the ethos within the school enabled it to be implemented relatively easily. Staff stated that they intended to continue using single-sex classes and were considering expanding the approach to pupils of all abilities within the year, but emphasised that it was important to consider the appropriateness of using single-sex classes in relation to the different groups of pupils.

Appendix 4.1

An example of target setting

EXAMPLES OF TARGETS AGREED BETWEEN PUPILS AND FORM TUTOR

1. **Target(s) set:**
   To achieve good results in all subjects. To have no detentions.
   Action Plan:
   To be more consistent in all lessons. To be less talkative.

2. **Target(s) set:**
   To improve attendance and punctuality.
   Action Plan:
   Must attend regularly.

3. **Target(s) set:**
   To improve the quantity and quality of homework.
   Action Plan:
   Do more than the bare minimum.
   Give all homework maximum effort. Check and correct when finished.

4. **Target(s) set:**
   To improve overall attitude to work in and out of school.
   Action Plan:
   Concentrate more fully.
   Do not allow myself to be distracted.
   Give homework and class work maximum effort.

5. **Target(s) set:**
   Improve confidence in lessons.
   Improve concentration in Spanish and Geography.
   Action Plan:
   Listen to teacher more carefully.
   Revise more thoroughly for tests.

6. **Target(s) set:**
   To improve the quality of homework and presentation of work.
   Action Plan:
   Do my homework on the day set, referring any problems to _____
   (Form Tutor).

Appendix 4.2

An example of a completed record sheet following a mentoring session

New Targets or Action to be taken before the next review
Attendance/Punctuality Maintain excellent punctuality & attendance. levels
Coursework/Subject Try harder in Maths to concentrate in class. Try to get maximum marks on all coursework for examinations
Personal 1. Get a part-time Job this Summer 2 Continue winning at Basketball.
Career Prepare for career interview! So that you can make the right decisions about what to do when you leave school.

Have your targets been met or are you on course to meet them?	
	✓ /X
1 **Attendance/Punctuality Targets** Excellent attendance + punctuality	✓
2 **Coursework/Subject Targets** Recording homework in logbook. Draw up a revision plan.	✓
3 **Personal Targets** Still need to find a part-time job. Joined a basketball team	X ✓
4 **Career Targets** Leisure industry is the area of work which appeals.	X

Comments (Progress - Evidence)

Attendance/Punctuality

Setting off earlier to drop brother off
So punctuality is better

Coursework/Subject

Revision timetable drawn up to help
with exams.
Homework now being entered in
logbook and being used more effectively.
(quite a number of credits awarded).

Personal

Still looking for a job in the area
but not much available locally.

Team now starting to win because you
are working more as a team.

Career

Researched jobs in school careers
library

Appendix 4.3

An example of a memo sent to subject teachers to involve them in the mentoring of pupils

---

YEAR 11 MENTORING PROGRAMME

FROM: _____

TO: _____

CONCERNING: _____   TUTOR GP:

_____

I shall be mentoring   _____ as part of the
Raising Standards Project. I shall be using the Student Planner as a key document
and would ask if you could keep a specific eye on him/her to ensure that all work/
homework is being recorded. If I can help you in working with this student in any
particular way please let me know.

Signature: _____

Appendix 4.4:

A copy of guidelines provided to staff mentors

Guidelines to Staff

Aim: The aim of the Year 11 Mentor Programme is to provide additional help and support for pupils so that they can succeed to the best of their ability in the final examinations.

These guidelines are to help you provide the best possible support for our students.

1. Please try to meet with your mentee on a regular basis. It is up to you to set a mutually convenient time.

2. It is the mentee's responsibility to record notes from the meeting and any targets set. Please check that pupil's are doing what they said they would.

3. During the meetings it is important to discuss progress and set targets. Possible areas for discussion may include homework, coursework, tests, revision, problems with subjects.

4. You may find yourself as the link between students, subject teachers, form tutors and parents. Talk to them about the progress of the student and do not hesitate to contact parents if you feel it is necessary.

5. Please keep all targets realistic. You will be provided with a summary of each mentee's progress so far plus regular updates to help you set realistically high targets.

6. It is important that a positive approach is taken at all times. Some students will be feeling the pressure and the job of the mentor is to help keep their morale as high as possible.

7. Pupils are being encouraged to work in support groups please encourage the development of a team ethos between your mentees by asking them about how they have supported each other in class, revision, coursework etc.

8. If you need any more advice or information please talk to, the Mentor Programme Co- ordinator, or Head of Year 11.

9. Please stress the importance of relaxation as well as work in the run up to the final examinations.

10. Thank you for your time and support. Together we will see an improvement.

11. At the end of the programme we will evaluate its success. If you have any comments please pass them on to the Mentor Programme Co-ordinator.

Mentor Programme Co-ordinator.

Appendix 4.5

One school's ideas about possible strategies mentors could use

POSSIBLE STRATEGIES MENTORS MIGHT USE!

1. Careful checking/discussion based on planners.

2. Planning of homework/coursework requirements into out of school time/ school time.

3. Methods of completing ongoing work effectively.

4. Revision Planner.

5. Revision techniques/strategies.

6. Time management strategies.

7. Quality of presentation.

8. Praise letters to parents.

9. Conversations with parents about ways they can help.

10. Broader discussion with students about issues which concern them, particularly after the mock exams.

11. Helping students plan for the future (careers etc).

12. Use of last report (Tutors have copies).

13. Encouragement of students to be involved in revision clubs/groups/activities in free time.

14. Contact with parents to discuss homework/revision strategies.

Appendix 4.6

A copy of a letter informing parents about the mentoring programme

ADDRESS

DATE

Dear *NAME*

XXXXX School has chosen to be included in a nationwide project aimed at supporting students with their learning as we move into the final phase of preparation for GCSE examinations. The project is designed particularly to support those students who are expected to achieve a range of examination results around the employment benchmark target of 5 grade 'C' GCSE passes. The purpose of the project is to work with individual students seeking to improve their performance.

At XXXXX school we are seeking to apply a range of approaches designed by Staff to improve the quality of learning for all students. One of these strategies is to allocate some students a 'mentor'. This will be a senior member of Staff who will meet regularly with the student to monitor and guide, encourage and support, providing a link between the student, XXXXX teachers and parents. We feel that XXXXX would particularly benefit from this individualised approach and, as a consequence, have arranged for XXXX to be "mentored" by XXXX. XXXX will be making contact with XXXX in the next few days and organising regular contact sessions to help XXXX make the best of *his/her* opportunities in the weeks to come. Obviously XXXX may wish to contact you directly, either by telephone or letters to discuss XXXX progress but if you would like to speak to XXXX at any point please do not hesitate to make contact via the School Office.

If you would like any further details and information about the work we are undertaking as part of this project please contact either the Headteacher, the Deputy Headteachers, me or XXXX mentor. We look forward to a successful project which will result in valuable progress leading up to the GCSE exams in the Summer.

Yours sincerely

Head of Year 11

Appendix 4.7

Staff-mentor questionnaire for evaluating a mentoring programme

Last year you volunteered to take part in the mentoring of Year 11 pupils. Whilst I realise that you have little time I would appreciate some feedback on how you felt the process went and ways that future programmes could be improved. To that end can you please complete the short questionnaire and return it to (*project co-ordinator*) as soon as possible.

1. How often did you meet with your mentees?

2. How did you arrange the times of the meetings?

3. Was each session structured?

4. Was each session at the same time every week?

5. If you mentored two people did you meet them separately?

6. Did you record any minutes of the meetings?

7. Did you feel that the process was effective in supporting your mentees?

8. How seriously did they take the process?

9. Did they follow the advice that they were given?

10. What do you feel was good about the mentoring process?
....

11. What do you feel was poor about the process?
....

12. What changes would you suggest to improve the process?
....

13. Would you volunteer to be a mentor on a future mentoring programme?

14. Do you feel the advice given was affected by the faculty that you work in?

15. Any further comments
....

Appendix 4.8

Pupil questionnaire for evaluating a mentoring programme

Last year after your mock exams you were enrolled on a mentoring programme. The school is about to re-introduce this programme into the current year 11 pupils. We want to improve how the system works and need your views in order to do this. Please spend a short time completing this questionnaire so that we know what you thought of the process.

1. How often did you meet with your mentor?

2. Was each session structured?

3. Was each session at the same time every week?

4. Did you follow the advice given by your mentor?

5. Did the support you were given help with:

Revision	[ ]
Building confidence	[ ]
Time Planning	[ ]
Coursework	[ ]
Exam techniques	[ ]

6. How seriously did you take the process?

7. Were you given the choice to be mentored?

8. Would you like to have been given a choice of mentor?

9. Did you feel the support given helped with success in the final exams?

10. Did you feel your mentor was there to help you or the school?

11. What do you feel were the good things about the mentoring process?

....

12. What do you feel were the poor things about the mentoring process?

....

13. Any further comments?

....

Appendix 4.9

A case study summary of a school that had implemented mentoring

Constable Lane was a 11 – 16 school. It was located in the suburbs of a city in the north-east of England and served a predominantly middle-class population. Senior members of staff conducted an investigation into boys' achievement and found significant differences between the performance of boys and girls, especially in terms of examination results. Staff considered different ways of tackling the issue on the basis that boys and girls have distinct learning styles which impact on their levels of performance. Staff therefore decided to introduce a mentoring programme in order to tackle the different weaknesses in pupils' learning styles, in the hope that it would raise achievement and address gender gaps in performance.

During the first year, staff decided to target Year 11 boys who were on the borderline of gaining five + A – Cs at GCSE as they felt that this would enable them to improve the school's overall level of achievement relatively easily. Following the success of the programme with this group, three complementary strands were introduced in the following year. One targeted Year 11 girls who were on the borderline of five + A – C and the other two targeted high-ability pupils – one for high-ability boys and one for high-ability girls. All four strands of the programme provided mentoring to pupils in small groups but they were all quite distinct as each tackled the specific weaknesses that these groups of pupils had. For example, the programme for borderline boys used peer pressure, competition and prizes to increase boys' levels of motivation and achievement. In contrast, the programme for borderline girls was based on the provision of fortnightly group meetings, which provided a forum for the girls to set targets and receive support and advice.

The pupils were chosen through analyses of previous test results. They were asked whether they wanted to participate in the programme, which was voluntary. If they agreed, the permission of their parents was sought. All staff within the school attended conference days on gender and achievement, but the four senior members of staff who coordinated the four different strands of the mentoring programme did not receive any additional training. Staff noted that during the first year of each of the different strands, there was a notable amount of extra work, effort and cost involved in operationalising the programme.

The efficacy of the different strands of the programme was monitored through questionnaires which were sent to pupils and their parents and through GCSE examination results. At the time of writing this report, findings were only available on the impact of the strand for borderline boys. These findings showed that pupils, parents and staff viewed the scheme as beneficial and there was a general improvement of ten per cent in the number of boys who gained five + A – Cs at GCSE, with 17 out of the 22 boys targeted (77 per cent) achieving five + A – C grades.

Staff felt that the strategy was successful because all staff were fully involved and committed and because it was presented to the targeted pupils in a positive way. Staff planned to continue working with similar groups of pupils but recognised that they had to be alert to the need to modify their approaches in the light of increased experience of addressing gender differences and the changing nature of each year group.

Appendix 5.1

A copy of a letter informing parents of child's participation in literacy support sessions

DATE

Dear Parent,

As part of our ongoing commitment to raising standards in reading, your child has been selected to take part in our Reading Task Force initiative. This involves being paired with an adult volunteer, for a minimum of at least three x half hour sessions a week.

The initiative will last until end of term, when another group of children will be chosen to benefit. If you do not wish your child to take part please let us know. The sessions will commence on week beginning Monday 22nd February.

Yours Faithfully,

Headteacher

Appendix 5.2

A copy of a letter informing parents of child's completion of literacy support sessions

DATE

Dear parents,

Your child has just completed the first of our Reading Task Force sessions. It has been a great success, due to the wonderful commitment of the volunteers. We are very grateful to them, and to you for allowing your child to take part.

A new cohort of children will be chosen for the next half term, but there is a possibility that your child will be chosen again at a later date. If this happens, you will of course be informed.

Yours sincerely

Headteacher

Appendix 5.3

A copy of a letter inviting parents to provide feedback on the use of literacy support sessions

DATE

Dear Parents

This will be the last week for the Reading Task Force before Christmas. We are holding a meeting on Tuesday 15th at 3.00 in school, for any feedback or suggestions you may have.

We would like to thank you all for your valuable time and support, and hope you will join us again after the Christmas break. Have a safe and happy holiday.

Yours sincerely

Headteacher

Appendix 5.4

A summary of pupils' reading scores at a case study school

The results of pupils who participated in the first block of sessions

Year group /gender	Reading age BEFORE half term block of sessions	Reading age AFTER half term block of sessions	DIFFERENCE in reading age
Y2 – male	6.0	6.0	0
Y2 – male	6.0	6.6	0.6
Y3 – female	6.6	7.6	1.0
Y3 – male	7.0	6.9	-0.1
Y4 – female	7.0	8.0	1.0
Y4 – male	7.3	8.0	0.7
Y5 – male	9.0	8.6	-0.4
Y5 – male	8.6	9.3	0.7
Y6 – male	9.3	10.9	1.6
Y6 – female	10.0	10.0	0

There was an average increase of 0.51 in reading age score for pupils who participated in the first block of reading sessions.

The results of pupils who participated in the second block of sessions

Year group /gender	Reading age BEFORE half term block of sessions	Reading age AFTER half term block of sessions	DIFFERENCE in reading age
Y2 – male	6.3	7.0	0.7
Y2 – female	6.3	6.3	0
Y3 – male	7.0	7.6	0.6
Y3 – male	6.9	7.9	1.0
Y4 – female	7.9	8.6	0.7
Y4 – male	11.6	12.9	1.3
Y5 – female	8.3	8.3	0
Y5 – male	9.6	12.3	2.7
Y6 – female	9.3	11.6	2.3
Y6 – male	9.3	9.3	0

There was an average increase of 0.93 in reading age score for pupils who participated in the second block of reading sessions.

Appendix 5.5

A case study summary of a school that had implemented additional literacy support

Callaghan Primary School was located in an inner city and served a predominantly working-class population. The headteacher was aware of national concerns regarding boys' underachievement, especially in literacy, and an analysis of NCA test results revealed that boys within the school were underachieving in literacy to a greater extent than girls. The headteacher therefore decided to implement a strategy that would enable underachieving pupils to gain a greater appreciation of literacy by spending more time reading. The school was located in a tight-knit community, so it was decided to build on the school's traditionally strong levels of parental involvement by asking parents to volunteer to provide additional literacy support. It was felt that by using non-teachers it would provide children with a pleasant environment that would encourage them to perceive reading as an enjoyable experience.

Staff from Years 2 to 6 were asked to select two pupils who they thought would benefit from taking part in the scheme. Therefore, at any one time, roughly ten pupils would be participating in the scheme. Initially, staff did not make a conscious decision to target boys specifically, but of the pupils whom they selected as those who would benefit most from the scheme, the large majority were boys. Staff thought it was important to inform all of the pupils about the programme as it was felt that over time most of the pupils would have an opportunity to participate in the scheme and it would reduce the possibility of targeted pupils receiving negative feedback from their peers. Once pupils were selected by class teachers, letters were sent out to their parents informing them about the strategy and asking for their permission to allow their child to participate.

The volunteer literacy supporters were not provided with any formal training. However, they were invited to attend a session where the headteacher explained to them the structure of the programme and what their role entailed, and an adviser from the LEA spoke to them about possible strategies that they could employ to help children with their reading. A new range of books also had to be purchased in order to increase the choice available to the children and to meet the interests of reluctant readers. In addition, the library had to be redecorated to create a welcoming reading environment.

Literacy supporters worked with children for half a term, on a one-to-one basis, for 20 minutes, three times a week. Their role was to help raise pupils' appreciation of reading through discussing texts and reading books of interest to the pupil. Sessions were scheduled to take place during lesson time, which meant that it was important for class teachers to work closely with the literacy supporters so that the teachers could ensure that the children did not miss out on anything essential. At the beginning and end of each half term block, the SENCO tested each of the participating pupils' reading ability.

The effectiveness of using literacy supporters was assessed through pupil reading tests and informal discussions with teachers, parents and supporters. Following two blocks of half-termly sessions, the scores from the children's reading tests showed that notable improvements had been made, although it was too soon for staff to say whether the targeted children would be able to maintain these gains. There was also a general feeling among teachers, parents and supporters that the sessions were benefiting pupils in terms of increasing their confidence in, and enthusiasm for, reading.

Staff felt that the main factors which contributed to the success of the strategy were the high levels of communication, enthusiasm and commitment from staff, parents and supporters. It was also important that the strategy was presented in a way that did not lead children to perceive it as targeted at specific pupils.